Budgies

Budgies

A Guide to Caring for Your Parakeet

By Angela Davids

photographs by Carolyn McKeone

BOWTIE
P R E S S ®

Irvine, California

Karla Austin, *Business Operations Manager*
Nick Clemente, *Special Consultant*
Barbara Kimmel, *Editor*
Jerry G. Walls, *Editor-at-Large*
Jill Dupont, *Production*
Michael V. Capozzi, *Design*
Indexed by Kenneth Brace

The budgies in this book are referred to as *he* or *she* in alternating chapters unless their gender is apparent from the activity discussed.

Photographs copyright ©2006 Carolyn McKeone. Photographs on pages 20, 31, 81, 94, 97, 123, 138-139, 164 © Isabelle Francais.
The budgies photographed for this book are courtesy of Pet Paradise, London, Ontario; Tristen Davis, Cindy George, Kim Hall, Carolyn A. McKeone, and Judy Walsh.

Library of Congress Cataloging-in-Publication Data

Davids, Angela.
  Budgies : a guide to caring for your budgie / by Angela Davids ; photographs by Carolyn McKeone.
    p. cm. — (Complete care made easy)
  ISBN 1-931993-70-X
  1. Budgerigar. I. Title. II. Series.

  SF473.B8D385 2006
  636.6'864—dc22

2005027943

BowTie Press®
A Division of BowTie, Inc.
3 Burroughs
Irvine, California 92618

Printed and bound in Singapore
10 9 8 7 6 5 4 3 2 1

Acknowledgments

I'D LIKE TO THANK JERRY G. WALLS, EXPERIENCED author and editor, for his groundwork and research for this book, particularly on the topics of breeding, genetics, and color variations.

—Angela Davids

For Charlie Rallo, Darryl Stacey, and John Noubarian, three great jazz musicians. Also, for Ed Bloor of Maggie's, London, Ontario, Canada; your music kept me alive when nothing else could.
Luv and thanks.

—Carolyn McKeone

Contents

1   Budgies in Nature and as Pets   8

2   Is a Budgie the Right Pet for You?   22

3   Selecting a Great Budgie   32

4   Basic Care of Your Budgie   46

5   The Proper Feeding of Budgies   68

6   Training Your Budgie   82

7   Keeping Your Budgie Healthy   98

8   The Basics of Breeding Budgies   124

9   Some Budgie Color Mutations   142

Appendix   159

Glossary   161

Index   165

1

Budgies in Nature and as Pets

Budgies have been highly sought-after pet birds since the mid-1860s, when they were brought from Australia to England and the European continent. Today, domestically bred budgies are one of the most popular pet birds in America.

MANY PEOPLE ARE SURPRISED AT HOW MUCH PERSONALITY can be packed into such a small bird! The colorful budgie—also widely known as a parakeet—is playful, energetic, entertaining, easy to train, and sometimes even talkative. It is no wonder that surveys often place the budgie as the most popular or the second most popular pet bird in American households.

Because of their small stature, budgies aren't always thought of as parrots, but they are. Parrots form a very large group, or order, of birds known as the Psittaciformes, which contains about 342 different bird species. The order is broken into two families: the Cacatuidae, or cockatoos; and the Psittacidae, the parrots. The term *parrot* can indicate either the family or the order. Some scientists believe there should be a third family, the Loriidae, containing just the lories and lorikeets.

Betcherrygah

WHEN THE FIRST ENGLISH EXPLORERS QUESTIONED THE Australian Aborigines about the local fauna, the explorers asked for the common names of the birds they saw, including the budgie. They were told that this abundant bird was called betcherrygah (sometimes spelled budgerygah). Further questioning led the explorers to interpret the word to mean "good bird." When the Aboriginal language was better understood, it was clear that good in this case meant good to eat.

There are many different names for the budgie. Scientists call this little Australian parrot *Melopsittacus undulatus*. Some historical references use the term *Australian shell parakeet*. About fifty years ago, another and more unusual name—budgerigar—began to appear often in books and articles about pet birds. Although this name sounds strange at first, its shortened form—budgie—rolls off the tongue with ease.

This book uses the term *budgie*, although many people still identify this bird as the parakeet. It is true that the budgie can be classified as *a* parakeet but certainly not as the only one. The term *parakeet* can apply to any member of the Psittacidae family who is relatively small, is slender, and has a long, pointed tail. Australia alone has more than two dozen species who fit under the general term *parakeet*, and many of the Mexican, South American, and Central American conures (also parrots) could be called parakeets on the basis of their size and shape. In southern Asia and Africa, several species of very long-tailed, bright green little parrots are also commonly known as parakeets.

Now let's get to know something about the budgie—the most popular parakeet of all.

The Wild Budgie

A wild budgie is a small, slender parrot with a pointed tail, pointed wings, and a small beak. The wild budgie is typically seven and a half to eight and a half inches long overall, with central tail feathers three and a half to four inches long (roughly

The Budgie's Scientific Classification

ALTHOUGH OFTEN CALLED A PARAKEET, THE BUDGERIGAR, or budgie, also has a scientific name that is standard among ornithologists, breeders, and pet owners around the world: *Melopsittacus undulatus.*
Class: Aves
Order: Psittaciformes
Family: Psittacidae
Genus: Melopsittacus
Species: undulatus

These budgies are resting together on a branch, just as budgies in the wild like to gather together in feeding and flying flocks.

half the bird's total length). The wings are long and pointed, with each wing roughly four inches long, so the wingspan is less than a foot. Wild budgies are much smaller but similar in structure to the American budgies, the birds you are likely to find in a pet store. American budgies are two to three inches smaller in length than the typical English budgies, who have been bred for competitive showing. The English budgies can be quickly identified by their large heads, which are round and bulging rather than small and tapered. (The English budgie is discussed in greater detail in chapter 9.)

Like other parrots, budgies can turn their heads 180 degrees so they can reach the important oil gland (the uropygial gland) at the upper base of the tail; budgies smear the oily secretions onto their beaks and then spread the oil over their feathers to make them more waterproof. A wet budgie thus keeps some dry plumage even during a rain storm or a light bath.

The budgie's beak is small, and its base is covered with feathers that can be fluffed out to enclose almost all but the tip of the beak. The upper beak is longer than the lower beak and is sharply pointed; the shorter lower beak fits into the upper beak and ends in a squarish tip. The tip of the lower beak fits against ridges in the upper beak that allow the budgie's thick, specialized tongue to roll an individual seed between the two parts of the beak until the outer coating is split and rolled off, thus hulling the seed before it is passed into the mouth and then down toward the stomach. Above the beak is a wide area of featherless skin that contains the nostrils. This area, called the cere, can vary in color, depending on the age and the sex of the bird.

A budgie's dark gray feet are large, with four unequal-size toes ending in large, sharp nails. The toes form an X (a pattern

All wild budgies have the green and yellow coloring you see here. This color pattern allows budgies to blend into their surroundings and thus avoid predators.

known as zygodactylous, common to all parrots), allowing the budgie to firmly grasp both large and small perches. The legs are short and mostly hidden under the feathers, giving the budgie a characteristic waddling walk.

Wild budgies are predominantly bright green, with yellow heads and throats and black feather markings—certainly not the variety of colors and shades you can find in a pet store. These limited colors allow wild budgies to blend with the colors of both the soils and grasses when they drop to the ground to feed. An adult bird is bright green from the upper chest to under the tail and on the rump (the part of the body above the base of the tail); the back, head, and neck are bright yellow. The body is heavily marked with black spots and crescents on the back and with many fine horizontal black lines on the nape of the neck and the back of the head. The face is bright yellow, with three large black spots on each side of the throat. The eyes are rather small, have whitish irises, and are surrounded by a narrow band of featherless skin, pinkish to bluish in color.

The tops of the wild budgie's wings are yellow and black, with green to black flight feathers (also called primaries); the undersides have a wide yellow bar and black primaries. The tail feathers are mostly blue-green and sometimes yellow on top, but the shorter feathers near the base are mostly yellow underneath; the central tail feathers are blue-green both on top and underneath.

Immature budgies differ little from adults, but from the time they leave the nest with their first set of feathers until they molt into their adult plumage (at about four months old), they can be distinguished by their somewhat duller colors, the absence or near absence of throat spots, and the continuation of the fine horizontal black lines from their napes over their crowns to the base of their beaks. If the crown and area above the beak are not one solid color, then the bird is almost certainly a baby. Young birds also have all-black eyes; the pupils become paler with age.

As mentioned, the budgies you see in a pet store may look quite different from the wild birds. Pets can be all yellow or all green, different shades of green or blue, or white, and the black markings may be faint or even nonexistent. Breeders have carefully and intentionally bred for these color varieties, which first appeared naturally as genetic mutations in pet birds; you'll never find them in nature. If a color mutation appeared in a wild budgie, the bird would stick out like a sore thumb in a flock of all green and yellow budgies and would attract predators; a short life span would reduce the likelihood of mating and passing on the mutation to any offspring.

Although a budgie's natural coloring is green and yellow only, pet budgies like these are available in a variety of colors and shades—including the normal (wild) green.

Range and Habitat

Budgies are strictly Australian birds. They gather in large flocks of dozens to thousands of birds who can be found almost anywhere in the dry interior plains of Australia and on the Indian Ocean shores of the continent. These birds do not tolerate even moderately wet habitats. Budgies occasionally appear in Tasmania, but those are thought to be escaped pets and not natural populations. Budgies truly are birds of deserts; extremely arid plains; and open, dry savannas with only sparse vegetation.

Because budgies are nomadic, it is difficult to pin down where any group of birds might be at any time of the year. The flocks move around constantly, following the rains; water is rare and rains are unpredictable, so grasses and other foods may not appear in one specific spot for several years. Flocks of thousands of birds may descend on shallow lakes that appear with annual rains. There they spend several weeks feeding on new grass and breeding. As is true for many other desert birds, the population numbers rise and fall depending on the weather—after many years of drought, a high percentage of budgies die, and the species may become relatively uncommon in an area; but the next extended period of rainfall and subsequent breeding season quickly return the species to normal numbers.

Feeding and Breeding

In nature, budgies feed on ripe and ripening seeds of a great array of grasses, especially the spinifex and Mitchell grasses that are common to the dry interior of Australia. But budgies also eat seeds of shrubby eucalyptus species and, in an emergency, will eat wheat and other cultivated crops. It is likely that wild budgies

Wild budgies are primarily seed eaters who feed on the ground. Your budgie may also happily munch on seeds and pellets placed in a cup on the cage floor.

will eat almost anything green or seedy if more traditional foods are not available.

Like most desert parrots, budgies are most active for an hour or less after sunrise and then for another hour or so before sunset, when temperatures are relatively low. Although they can survive temperatures over one hundred degrees Fahrenheit for a while, they are stressed by such extremes and do much better in ranges from the upper sixties to the low eighties. When winter comes, budgies often move to warmer climates, although they can (stressfully) tolerate temperatures as low as the mid-forties for a considerable time.

The unpredictability of food and water in the wild dictates budgies' breeding habits. Their young leave the nest and mature early, compared with other parrots, as an adaptation for survival; if the adult birds had to incubate the eggs and feed the chicks for months instead of weeks, the water and grasses would probably disappear before the nestlings could fly.

Wild budgies nest primarily during the periods when rains and food are most likely to be abundant, but nesting seasons are unpredictable. Birds from the northern part of the range often breed at a different time from those in the south because climate patterns in Australia usually produce rains at different times in these areas. Unlike many other nomadic Australian parrots, budgies seldom approach the eastern coast during the winter, so they are seldom found in major Australian cities.

Like almost all other parrots, budgies lay their white eggs in a hole in a rotting branch or tree trunk and don't bother to line the nest with straw or feathers. And, as is true of other parrots (but not cockatoos), the male feeds the female during nesting, and she seldom leaves the nest to look for food until the chicks are fairly grown and able to maintain their own body temperatures.

From Australia to England to America

The first Australian birds made their way to England on the ships of Captain James Cook, an English explorer who traveled to the

Budgies and cockatiels—other small parrots native to Australia—sometimes form mixed flocks in the wild, traveling together to find food and water.

eastern coast of Australia in the 1770s. Naturalists and others traveling with Cook collected a few birds and other animals and brought them back to Europe. These extremely rare specimens drew lots of interest from British and other European scientists, who named them according to the recently formulated rules of Linnaeus, a Swedish botanist who revolutionized taxonomy (the naming and classification of plants and animals).

On the basis of travelers' descriptions of a small green and yellow bird found in New South Wales on the southeastern coast of Australia, British naturalist George Shaw named the budgie *Psittacus undulatus*—a parrot (all parrots were placed in the genus *Psittacus*) with fine undulate (wavy) lines over the back and nape of the neck.

The first live budgies were brought to England in 1838 by painter John Gould, who not only visited Australia but also had family contacts there. Gould put budgies in a new genus, *Melopsittacus* (singing parrot), because of their melodious whistles or warbles. This gave us the current name *Melopsittacus undulatus*.

Gould and his friends and business associates soon were importing more budgies into England and elsewhere in Europe, where they found ready buyers among upper-class hobbyists willing to exchange gold for these new additions to their cages and aviaries. Budgies caused a sensation among fanciers wanting rare, expensive animals for their collections, and it wasn't long before budgies were being bred in high numbers in captivity. Imports continued into Europe until 1894, when Australia passed regulations forbidding further exportation.

Breeding budgies became a very profitable business in France, Holland, Belgium and Germany, countries that long had

All-yellow budgies, like this one, and all-blue budgies were all the rage in early twentieth-century America.

traditions of commercially raising many types of unique pets. Budgies commanded high prices, and if you were a banker or a duke or had similar stature, you had to have a pair to keep up with your friends. When an all-yellow budgie mutation appeared in Belgium in 1875, followed by blue mutations in the early 1880s, interest in these birds grew, and prices for the mutations often reached well into three figures. The blue birds proved especially popular in Japan after they were imported by a Japanese prince in 1925.

Budgies had reached the United States by the late 1920s, where they became extremely popular. Soon every home had to have a little cage with a budgie (preferably all blue or all yellow) sitting in it. Books about how to care for budgies were published, budgies appeared in print ads, and talking budgies even appeared on radio shows. They became even more popular in the 1950s, when they competed with canaries as the most popular pet birds.

Today, budgies can be found in more than twenty color mutations, and perhaps as many as one hundred varieties are widely available to breeders and pet bird owners, although most of those seen in pet shops are either yellow, green, blue, white, or green and yellow (as in the wild). No matter what color, all budgies have great pet potential and are relatively inexpensive to purchase and care for. By buying a budgie, you join hundreds of thousands of dedicated pet bird owners who have found budgerigars to be truly wonderful pet parrots.

2

Is a Budgie the Right Pet for You?

Once you've decided a bird is the pet for you, you will find a delightful companion in a budgie. And after you've seen how enjoyable one bird is, you may want two!

MANY FIRST-TIME PARROT OWNERS ARE SURPRISED AT the amount of care, time, and money a pet bird requires. Some people believe that a pet bird simply sits passively in a cage all day and is content as long as he receives regular food and water. In truth, parrots are highly intelligent, extremely social creatures who crave regular interaction, need a specialized diet, and require regular veterinary care. You'll discover that caring for a pet bird isn't much different than caring for a cat or dog. But first, ask yourself the following questions before welcoming a budgie in to your home.

Can you afford the time it takes to care for a budgie? You will need to feed your bird each morning and evening and replace his water every day. You also will need to spot-clean his

Your budgie will want a lot of your time and attention, and he will reward you with years of companionship.

cage, toys, and perches daily and do a thorough cleaning every week or two weeks. Budgies have high metabolisms and produce feces approximately every ten to fifteen minutes. Although many cages have seed guards, or aprons, around the edges to help funnel droppings, food crumbs, and seed hulls back into the cage, some debris will certainly escape. If you believe that vacuuming, sweeping, and dusting are dreaded chores, then a budgie—or any pet bird—probably isn't right for you.

Do you or does anyone in your household have allergies? Birds constantly shed small flakes of skin and secretions from around their feathers, and they spread dried dust from droppings, pelleted foods, and seeds. Some people are just as allergic to birds as others are to cats or dogs. Although allergies can be treated and are seldom severe, dealing with them certainly would be an added expense and nuisance.

Can you afford the time to give your bird at least an hour of one-on-one attention each day, along with a few hours of ambient attention, such as spending time in the same room, talking to the budgie, and supervising his playtime on top of the cage or on a playgym? Budgies are among the most human-centered pet birds and will become depressed if simply placed in their cages and ignored. Budgies need company because they are flock animals that in nature are never alone—other birds are near them when they fly, feed, sleep, and even nest. A lonely budgie may pick his feathers and tear his skin into bleeding patches; he won't eat and will become withdrawn and morose. As his owner, you are part of his flock, and he will demand your attention for as many hours a day as you can manage. Can you put down your work or set aside hobbies and housework so you can interact with your bird every day?

Are you willing to forego long vacations or even overnight visits to keep your bird company? Or are you willing to find and pay a bird sitter to watch your budgie when you *do* go away for business or vacation? Or do you have a trusted friend or neighbor who likes birds and would be willing to come by each day to spend time with your bird and refresh his food and water?

Are you prepared for the financial responsibilities of caring for a budgie? A safe, quality cage will cost more than the bird, although the cage should last for years. And you will be amazed at how many accessories you can buy to make your bird more comfortable or your cleaning efforts easier. You'll also have the ongoing expense of a high-quality food, as well as new toys and perches to replace those that become dirty and worn. One or two budgies are not expensive birds to maintain, but accidents and illnesses do happen, requiring veterinary visits and surprisingly large bills for such small birds. Can you budget for both the expected and the unexpected?

Will your neighbors tolerate a bird in your home? For that matter, are there local laws against keeping budgies? Some cities and states have passed laws that exclude all or most exotic pets, and budgies are still considered exotic in some places (even though they have been bred in captivity for a century and a half).You probably won't have any problems, but if you live in a large city such as Chicago or New York City, it is best to check for recent changes in the laws.

Apartment complexes and condominium developments often exclude pets of all types on the basis that they are a potential bother to neighbors. Budgies have relatively soft voices for parrots, but they can still call and whistle fairly loudly, and this can carry. If you suspect there will be a noise problem, check with

How Delicate Are Budgies?

ALL BIRDS ARE RELATIVELY DELICATE COMPARED with mammals. You need to be aware of the following physical characteristics before you purchase a budgie.

- Budgies have complex respiratory systems that require the ribs to move in and out when they breathe. Holding a budgie too tightly will restrict his breathing and could lead to death, as could exposing him to any potentially toxic fumes, such as those created by household cleaners or cigarette smoke.
- Their bones are hollow and fragile and contain extensions of the lungs, so a broken bone not only affects the bone but also leaves the lungs open to infections and bleeding.
- Birds bleed easily around the bases of feathers that are erupting through the skin (called pinfeathers, blood feathers, or feather shafts). If these feathers are injured, the bleeding can sometimes be hard to stop.
- Birds also have fewer fat reserves to tide them over if they miss a meal or suffer minor ailments, and often they show signs of diseases only just before dying.
- Budgies react wildly to sudden movements and even loud noises. Their typical reaction is to try to fly away from the disturbance, which can lead to deadly collisions with cage bars, toys, windows, or furniture.

The fact is that budgies are small, lightweight, relatively delicate pets who, at the same time, enjoy being handled and petted. Just keep this in mind: always handle your budgie gently, and avoid approaching his cage suddenly.

the owners or the management before making the investment in a pet that you may painfully have to give up later. Plainly put, responsible bird owners obey the law and respect their neighbors.

Do you or any other members of your family smoke? If so, a parrot isn't the pet for you. First, birds have highly efficient lungs

Budgies shouldn't be left alone with young children, but responsible older children can make good caretakers and playmates for birds such as these English budgies.

that allow them to take in oxygen rapidly and process it more thoroughly than, for instance, a mammal does. As birds take in oxygen, they take in any other compounds in the air, including secondhand smoke. Exposure to smoke of any kind can lead to respiratory disease and early death. Pet birds are also negatively affected by the exposure to nicotine and other chemicals that remain on a smoker's hands. When a smoker pets his or her bird, or when a bird perches on a smoker's finger, these toxins are transferred to the bird. The bird's feathers and feet become irritated, leading to highly destructive feather picking and intense foot chewing.

Budgies and Kids

Do you have young children in the home? Budgies are good pets for children, but only under an adult's supervision. These birds need to be fed twice a day, every day, which most children under twelve may not be able do consistently without guidance. And you can expect only the most responsible child to change a budgie's cage papers regularly without prompting from an adult.

Safety is another concern. Children may accidentally injure a budgie, perhaps by grabbing him tightly or throwing him when surprised by the bird's quick nip or scratch. Talk with your child about how to hold a budgie, what kinds of behaviors to expect (like small nips or taps of the beak), and how to respond. But be prepared to always supervise playtime between children and budgies.

Budgies and Other Pets

Do you share your home with other pets? If you have fish in an aquarium or perhaps a lizard in a terrarium, you'll have no problems. However, if you have cats, dogs, or even other pet birds, there is a potential for conflicts. Budgies cannot share their cages with larger birds, and even relatively small lovebirds and cockatiels may pick on budgies, pulling out feathers and trying to nip at their toes and eyes. Snakes are a no-no, of course, as most would regard a budgie as a great snack, and snakes escape from their cages often enough to simply not be safe to keep in the same house as a budgie.

Dogs sometimes adapt to having a budgie around the house, and many will ignore a bird or even treat him with gentle respect. However, even the smallest breeds of dog (who are more likely to chase a hopping or low-flying budgie than larger breeds are) can kill a budgie with a single snap of the jaws or by a scratch. Some people have had success gradually introducing (and always supervising) dogs and budgies, but it certainly cannot be recommended without caution.

These birds have been carefully introduced to these furry companions, who all got along nicely for this photograph. But always make sure your bird is supervised if you allow feather and fur interaction!

Cats are even more dangerous—any cat who deserves the name will look at a budgie as either prey or toy, and if the cat can reach him, the bird will be killed. Cats have sharp teeth and nails, all of which can wound a budgie with just a touch. And the bacteria carried by a cat's teeth and nails quickly produce infections that will kill most slightly wounded birds within a few days. Cats and budgies are a fatal combination.

Guinea pigs and rabbits may adapt to having a budgie around when both are free in a safe room, but they are clumsy enough to accidentally trample a budgie. Hamsters, rats, and mice may consider budgies prey—or at least worth a curious nibble that could have disastrous results. A curious budgie who is investigating a caged small mammal may become tangled in the bars of the cage or react in fright to a sudden movement in the cage, causing the bird to panic and inadvertently jump or fly into a wall, window, or furniture.

These warnings aren't meant to discourage you; they're just to give you a realistic picture of what pet bird ownership is like. Think carefully about how owning a bird will affect your household before rushing out to buy a budgie.

If your lifestyle can support a bird, a budgie will be one of the most rewarding pet companions you've ever known.

3

Selecting a Great Budgie

Here is an alert and healthy budgie—a good choice for a pet. Don't make a hasty decision when you purchase a bird; take the time to carefully select a healthy and happy individual.

ONCE YOU HAVE DECIDED THAT A BUDGIE IS THE PET FOR you, it's easy to get caught up in the excitement and purchase the first budgie who catches your eye. Before you bring that budgie home, though, be sure you have thought about what you are really looking for in a pet bird. Color, gender, age, and health are just are few aspects to consider.

Choosing a Color

A large pet store is sure to have an array of colored budgies, ranging from solid white to solid yellow or solid blue, with all shades of yellow, green, and blue in between. Does color make a difference in the quality of a pet? Probably not, as long as you plan to buy one of the common colors; some rare varieties have

This is a beautiful blue female budgie. What color you choose is a purely personal decision, as any healthy and well-handled budgie has the potential to be a great pet.

more health problems and may have shorter average life spans. It is highly unlikely, however, that any rare and problematic budgies will be available in your local pet store. Instead, you will find birds in the typical colors and shades, all of whom are similar in behavior, health, and longevity.

Choosing the Sex

There are differences in behavior between the sexes of budgies, although none really makes one a better pet than the other. Males tend to be outgoing compared with many females, and they whistle and sometimes talk better. This is to be expected, since a male is constantly trying to woo a female to mate, and the quality of his calls certainly affects how a potential mate perceives his desirability. Males often form very close bonds with their owners, even to the point of trying to feed them.

Females form bonds with their owners that can be just as strong as those of males. Many females are not quite as vocal as males are, however, although they may still whistle well. Females

There aren't many distinguishing features between this male and female budgie other than size and cere color. Males may be more likely to learn to talk than females will be, but both will learn to bond with you, given enough time and attention.

can be taught to speak, but fewer females are likely to speak as clearly as males do. Of course, there are exceptions to every rule, and speaking ability is often the result of an individual owner's training efforts. Remember that any speaking budgie talks rapidly in a very high voice that is difficult to understand, even at its best.

Adult females sometimes lay eggs even when no male is present, and they will try to incubate these infertile eggs. It is also possible for a female budgie to become egg bound, a condition in which the egg is trapped inside the bird's cloaca. Causes can include insufficient muscle tone or a diet lacking in calcium and other minerals that allow a thick shell to form around the egg. An egg-bound bird is listless, sits fluffed in a corner, and does not eat or drink. If you suspect egg binding, call your bird's veterinarian immediately; egg binding can be fatal.

One Budgie or Two?

If you are a first-time budgie owner, start by purchasing a single budgie. One bird will give you an idea of what it is like to have budgies as pets and whether you want to expand your bird family. Allow your first bird at least three or four months to become acclimated to you and your home and to undergo basic training and bonding. Once the first bird is fully bonded to you, it is okay to purchase a companion bird. Don't immediately put the second budgie (preferably a young bird) into the cage with the first one; instead, cage her separately near the first bird so the two have a few days or even weeks to get to know each other. Introduce them gradually, perhaps in a neutral room or on a new playgym, and only under your supervision. Female budgies are more agressive than male budgies are, so never place two females together in the same cage. So when you are deciding which sex to buy, just

It's hard to resist a baby as adorable as this one! But you should make sure your budgie is fully weaned and on an adult diet before you bring her home.

Fledglings

BUDGIES MATURE QUICKLY, AND YOU SHOULD BE certain the bird you choose is weaned before you buy her. A bird who is not fully weaned won't be able to eat the adult diet you offer her. At best, her development could be delayed; at worst, she could become sick and die.

Budgies typically wean when six to eight weeks old, but ask the breeder or store employee about the weaning status of your budgie, and make sure you see her actually eating adult food. Better yet, make arrangements to select your perfect pet bird and leave her at the pet store for one to two weeks before picking her up. This gives the store time to make sure the bird is weaned and allows you plenty of time to buy and set up the proper cage and accessories.

remember that if you put a male and a female together, you will get eggs, so two males may be the best pairing for pet budgies.

Where to Buy Your Bird

Most large pet stores always have at least a few budgies for sale, and some pet superstores may offer more than a dozen birds in a variety of colors. Pet stores that specialize in pet birds will offer you the best selection of all.

Not all pet stores are equal, and it is important to check the appearance of a store and the health of its birds before you consider buying a budgie there. Judge each store individually. Most shops are clean, but occasionally you will find one that doesn't meet even minimal standards. You have to make some allowances for the messy nature of birds, which is especially noticeable when a few birds are housed together in a store. If birds are overcrowded with no room for toys or to exercise, consider that a red flag. Because so many avian diseases are transmitted through the air, it is never safe to buy a budgie from a pet store that is questionably clean.

Ask to be allowed into the back of the store to see how the birds are fed and handled—good stores should let you see how they handle their birds. Ask the management and employees about budgies; do they really know about the birds, or do they give out bad information or ignore you? The best stores often have friendly and helpful employees, and the worst have truly disagreeable employees. Be sure to ask about the exact ages of the birds being sold: if the budgies have not yet been weaned, you will have to hand-feed your bird yourself, which can endanger her health if you aren't experienced at hand-feeding.

All reputable pet stores will offer some type of guarantee that covers the health of the bird for at least a few days after she leaves the shop—certainly long enough for you to take her to a veterinarian for a general examination. Make sure the store will take the bird back if the veterinarian finds a problem.

Keep in mind that a pet store isn't the only source for finding a budgie. Reputable breeders also have healthy birds, and pet bird owners and bird clubs are excellent sources for recommendations. When you visit a breeder's home or aviary, look for cleanliness, toys in the cages, healthy food, and plenty of room in the cages for the budgies to hop and flutter about. Ask the breeder about his or her experience with budgies, and confirm that he or she will be available to answer any questions you have *after* you take your bird home.

Budgies are sometimes available for adoption from animal shelters or through bird rescue groups. See the appendix for a list of parrot rescue organizations.

Find a Healthy Bird

Under no circumstances should you buy a budgie from a pet store or breeder's aviary where there are sick birds—the chances of infection spreading are too likely. Make sure the budgies are active, have bright and clean eyes, and are walking or fluttering around in the cages. They should not be sitting still in a corner with their heads hidden in their feathers unless it is their normal nap time. Ask to inspect individual birds while they're being held by a store employee so you can touch the birds and look carefully at all their features.

First check the head. The eyes should be bright and clean and not be sunken into the face. Young budgies' eyes are virtually all blackish brown; as they mature, a gray iris ring develops around each black pupil, becoming whitish in adults (although this is not true for some color mutations). The beak should be well formed, never asymmetrical, with a sharp upper point and a lower point that fits correctly into the upper beak. Give the bird a seed and see how it is handled; if the bird has problems hulling the seed, there is something wrong with either the beak or the tongue. There must also be no mucus on the nostrils, which could indicate a respiratory infection.

The feathers of the body should be correctly formed and lie flat, without bare spots or twisted feathers. (In an immature budgie, it is normal for the area over the crop to have exposed skin between the feathers.) The feathers around the vent must be clean, with no signs of diarrhea. Central tail feathers should be straight and not badly broken or twisted; damage from being in a small cage will usually be corrected with the next molt, but sometimes twisted tail feathers are an ongoing problem.

This is the head of a healthy young bird. The cere is clean, the eyes are bright and dark, and the beak is nicely formed.

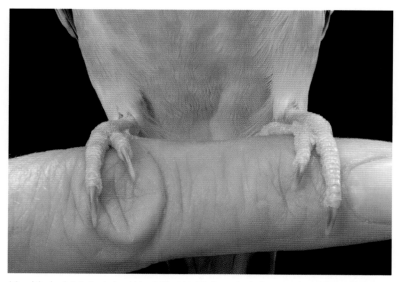

A healthy budgie's feet should look like this bird's—relatively smooth and free of lumps or sores, with fully formed toes and a nail on each toe.

There should be good muscling on either side of the sternum (the bird's breast bone), and the wings should be strong when they are flapped. A budgie with drooping wings may be sick.

Examine the droppings on the bottom of the cage. Healthy budgie droppings will be uniform in consistency and appearance and won't be runny. Loose droppings are the result of diarrhea, which can be a symptom of many illnesses. Be particularly cautious of bright yellow or lime green droppings, which could indicate the presence of disease; but keep in mind that the color of the droppings is greatly influenced by the color of the foods being eaten.

Check the feet and legs. The skin should be clean (no packed feces at the folds or under the feet) and without sores. Young budgies have relatively smooth skin on their legs and feet, whereas old birds often have many naturally rough spots. There should be no obviously enlarged bulges on the toe joints that indicate infection or damage. The nails should be present on all the toes and must not be twisted; if they are long, the store employee should be able to show you how to trim them correctly. Budgies' feet are very important because budgies are ground-feeding birds who spend a lot of time walking around. Healthy feet also allow the bird to get a proper grip on a perch. If the budgie seems to have problems holding onto a perch and the perch is of the proper diameter, then something is likely to be physically wrong with the bird.

Check the Personality

A budgie's initial disposition toward people may depend on how she is raised: parent-raised, hand-raised, or hand-fed. Her price

A Visit to the Veterinarian

PLAN TO TAKE YOUR NEW PET TO A VETERINARIAN FOR A checkup as soon as possible. A veterinarian can see problems you won't notice and can give you a general evaluation of the bird's health. In many areas, the store's warranty will not be valid unless the budgie is examined by a veterinarian. There are usually time limits on warranties, generally from a couple of days to a week.

Veterinarians are trained medical professionals, and you should plan to spend perhaps three hundred to five hundred dollars (depending on the city) for a complete veterinary workup. This may sound expensive for a bird who is likely to cost from twenty to seventy-five dollars, but it is essential for your pet's long and healthy life. You'll need to budget for this veterinary cost, as well as for annual checkups.

Budgies have different personalities just as they have different coloring, as this group demonstrates. Look for a bird who's easily approachable and whose personality seems to fit yours.

will also vary depending on how she was raised, given the increased amount of time it takes to hand-feed and handle a bird.

Parent-raised (and therefore parent-fed) budgies may not be tame unless the pet store or breeder has been making a solid effort to tame them. They may be hesitant to step up onto your finger and may not enjoy being petted. Some budgie owners do not mind buying untamed budgies and are happy to tame them themselves. (See chapter 6 for information on taming and training.)

Hand-raised budgies are fed by their parents until weaning, at which time the pet store or the breeder actively gets the birds used to being handled by humans by interacting with them several times every day. Hand-fed budgies are fed by a human at some point before weaning; some may be fed by hand from the beginning, and others may be fed by the parents at first and then fed by hand for the last few weeks of weaning. Some people use the terms *hand-raised* and *hand-fed* interchangeably, so ask pet store employees or breeders exactly what they mean when they use either term.

The best way to judge the personality of an individual bird is to observe her and then handle her yourself, perhaps over several visits to the pet store or breeder's aviary. Approach the cage slowly, allow the bird to come close to the front of the cage, and then extend your finger just in front of the bird's belly, providing a perch. You may also use your thumb as a perch, and then gently wrap your hand around the bird to lift her. If you feel comfortable handling her and she seems comfortable and interested in being handled by you, you've found your match.

It's Your Decision

Every pet bird owner has different opinions on what makes the best budgie. But you won't go wrong if you buy a healthy, weaned budgie, preferably slightly immature or a very young adult (older birds may be difficult to bond with), of whatever color and sex you prefer.

Budgies live five to eight years on average, with some reaching twelve to fifteen years of age. This means your pet may be with you for about a decade. Choose wisely!

4

Basic Care of Your Budgie

Although the cage is your bird's haven while you are away from home, a well-socialized budgie will relish the time spent interacting with you once you return.

THE MOST IMPORTANT THING YOU CAN DO TO HELP YOUR budgie feel comfortable in his new home is to buy and set up the cage *before* you bring him home. After traveling in a dark cardboard box or small travel cage, your bird may be nervous and upset, and he will welcome the comfort of a cage well equipped with fresh water, the food he is accustomed to, a couple of toys, and a few perches of various diameters. When you get home, put your budgie into his new cage, and leave him untouched for a day or two as he gets used to the new cage and the sounds around it. A few times each day, approach the cage slowly, talk to your budgie, and make eye contact. For the first couple of days, don't try to put your fingers or hands into the cage—just let his cage be his castle!

The Cage

Before buying the cage, consider not only its size but also its construction. Not every cage will work for a budgie, and not every pet store that sells budgies also sells cages appropriate for budgies.

Cage Size

The cage will be the most expensive item you purchase for your budgie, so you will want to do it only once. Plan to buy a high-quality cage that is safe, will last, and is as large as you can afford—and will fit in your home. A single budgie needs a cage that measures a minimum of eighteen inches long, wide, and tall, although a cage at least twenty-four inches long will allow even more room for your budgie to roam. If you think you may purchase a second budgie in the future, consider twenty-four inches the minimum length, and go up to thirty inches if you can. If you buy a large cage, be sure the bars are spaced no more than a half-inch apart. Otherwise, curious budgies may try to work their heads in between the bars and get stuck.

Cage Shape and Construction

A relatively low, long cage will suit a budgie's ground-feeding habits, and a tall one will offer plenty of climbing opportunities. Budgies don't need ornamentation on their cages; fancy scrollwork and turrets are just traps for a budgie's feet and may even mask weak spots in the cage construction. Parrots, including budgies, need many horizontal bars on the sides of the cages because they use their feet and beaks to grasp the bars and climb around. Cages meant for canaries and other finches have few horizontal bars because these birds don't climb the way parrots

Budgies are active birds, and they will take advantage of climbing and swinging opportunities if given the right perches and swings.

do, so avoid canary cages. Round cages also are designed for canaries and are not suitable for budgies, who like to have corners into which to retreat. The cage should be designed to be placed on a firm foundation, not hung from the ceiling or a stand; budgies don't like swaying cages.

Many cages sold are actually dangerous for your bird, so check their construction carefully. Make sure all weld spots are firm and preferably out of the budgie's reach. If there is any lead in the weld and the bird chews it, he will quickly suffer from heavy metal poisoning, leading to death. Cages made of chrome or brass can also be dangerous; if the metal flakes off when chewed, the budgie will ingest the toxic metal.

Avoid any cage with bars covered in cheap rubber or plastic that could be chewed off and swallowed. These cages are usually small and inexpensive—and you get what you pay for. The same is true of cages made of galvanized wire; they are low in cost but can be high in metal toxicity.

Instead, look for either a stainless steel cage or a wrought iron cage with powder-coated paint. This type of paint creates a durable, long-lasting barrier between the metal and your budgie's beak. An epoxy coating is another safe way to cover cage bars.

Cages made of Plexiglas or heavy acrylic plastics on the top and two sides are also available. These cages may become warm

Seed Guards

MOST CAGES TODAY COME WITH WIDE STRIPS OF RIGID plastic or aluminum, about two to three inches high, that fit outside the cage just above the rim of the bottom pan. These seed guards help keep seed hulls and pellet crumbs inside the cage and prevent the droppings from escaping. Some cage designs have fixed guards, whereas others allow you to remove the guards for regular cleaning and to replace them when needed.

Like this bird, your budgie will enjoy time spent out of the cage. Just make sure the decision is yours—and not your bird's—by ensuring that the cage door fits securely!

in the summer and a bit moist during humid weather, but otherwise they last forever (but take care during cleaning, as acrylics scratch easily). Because a budgie wants to climb on all four sides of the cage, however, this type is perhaps more suitable as a temporary cage to be used to take your budgie to the veterinarian or to isolate him during a spell of ill health.

The cage must have a securely fitted door that is large enough to allow the bird (and your hand, if necessary) to enter and leave easily. A small door will make cleaning the cage difficult and is likely to bend the budgie's tail feathers when he enters or exits the cage.

Budgies are intelligent birds and are more powerful than you may think. They can attack a simple door latch and either damage it or release it. Doors that hinge from the bottom and latch at the top are the most dangerous; if the bird opens the latch, the door will pop open, and the bird can escape. Examine the latch carefully, and make sure your bird will not be able to open the door. If in doubt, use a small padlock made of nontoxic materials to be certain that the cage stays shut and that your bird isn't harmed by chewing on it.

Most cages today have one of two types of bottoms: a plastic base that serves as the cage bottom and that may have a removable tray; or a grate with a tray underneath that slides in and out. Of the two types, the second is preferred because the cage is sturdier and easier to clean.

The bottom of the cage can be lined with paper, either heavy unprinted paper or newspaper, for easy cleaning. The paper should be absorbent, of course, to handle the liquid in the droppings; paper towels are another good choice. Some people like the look of bird-safe substrates made of corncob or recycled paper, but these are optional. Never use cat litter, which is extremely dusty and may cause harm if ingested.

Cage Placement

Place your budgie's cage on a solid, immobile surface, such as a table or a special cage stand. Don't use an upright rod with hanging hooks to suspend the cage. Such hooks seldom are truly secure, and they allow the cage to move when people walk by, which is sure to disturb or even panic your budgie. Stick with a table that places the top of the cage at about eye level; budgies don't like people to approach them from above, the way predatory birds would attack them. Many owners believe that a budgie feels more secure if the back of the cage is

Place the cage where your budgie will be able to hear and see the activity in the house. The cage should be in a draft-free area and somewhere where it is quiet at night.

placed in front of a wall or other unmovable surface, so at least one side is protected from what the budgie may view as approaching predators.

Where should you place the cage? A budgie is part of your family and wants to be part of the action going on around him—he doesn't want to be in an empty bedroom or dark closet all day. Look for an area where there is opportunity for human contact from morning through evening, where people going by can talk to the bird and interact with him. A bird in a neglected room becomes a neglected bird.

Unfortunately, the kitchen, one of the most popular rooms in the home, is also one of the most dangerous. The list of things in a kitchen that can kill or harm a budgie seems endless—everything from a hot stove and hot water faucets to common kitchen chemicals such as soaps, cleansers, and cooking sprays. Cooking in a pan with a nonstick coating can release vapors that quickly affect the respiratory system of a bird and cause death. People once believed that a nonstick surface had to be heated above five hundred degrees Fahrenheit before releasing the dangerous vapors of the synthetic polymer polytetrafluoroethylene (simply called PTFE), but there have been documented cases in which normal heating over an extended period caused the death of pet birds. Why take the risk?

The family room is a good place if you are sure you can keep the room quiet in the late evening when the bird needs to sleep. Budgies don't like loud, sudden noises, but they can get used to a lot of normal background noise over time. Perhaps a home office, where you work each day and can take a few

Keep 'Em Cozy

AVOID DIRECT DRAFTS FROM AIR CONDITIONERS AND partially opened windows during cold weather. Avoid positioning your budgie directly in front of your heating system as well, and an outside door that is opened and closed many times a day during cold winter months can drastically change the room's temperature.

minutes out of your schedule every few hours for some one-on-one time, might work best; but don't neglect the bird when you aren't working.

Cage Accessories

A cage is just a cage without the proper accessories, which turn it into a home for your budgie. Some of the following accessories will probably come with the cage you purchase, but don't hesitate to upgrade your budgie's humble home.

Food Cups

Many cages sold today have openings, or ports, in the sides where small plastic food cups can be inserted into the cage from the outside (so you don't have to open the door). Avoid cages that leave space around the food cups where a budgie could get stuck. Check the fit of the food cups, and make sure they are tight. Then check the type of plastic the cups are made of—avoid flimsy cups your budgie can easily chew, as virtually all plastics are dangerous to budgies if swallowed. If you are unsure about

These are just some of the accessories available for your budgie's cage: food and water cups, cuttlebones, and toys. Other must-haves include perches of varying diameters.

the safety of the cups that came with the cage, replace the cups right away.

The best and certainly safest choice for budgie food cups are those made of stainless steel. This material is resistant to chewing, does not rust, is hard to dent even when dropped from heights, and lasts through thousands of cleanings. Because inexpensive plastics are porous, they absorb stains and often retain a slimy film coating even after washing. Some very hard, thick plastics are better and are certainly durable enough for a budgie's small beak. Whether you buy steel or heavy plastic cups, you may want to buy a few extra for replacements and to use when you are cleaning the original cups.

If the cage has no cup ports, look for stainless steel cups with holders that can be securely attached to the bars of the cage. Many cups of this type fit into metal harnesses that screw onto the cage bars. Make sure the harnesses are not made of cheap iron coated with chrome that can flake off and become a health hazard. Some thick plastic cups have stems that fit through the bars and are held in place by heavy nuts on the other side; these cups are sturdy and not easily chewed by budgies.

Each budgie in a cage will need his own food cup to prevent squabbles. Never place food cups under perches where the birds' droppings could land in the cups. And budgies prefer to feed near and on the ground, so don't place the food cups too high in the cage.

Water Cups

The same guidelines that apply to food cups also apply to water cups. In fact, the two types are interchangeable, and stainless steel is always best. Again, position the cups so there is little

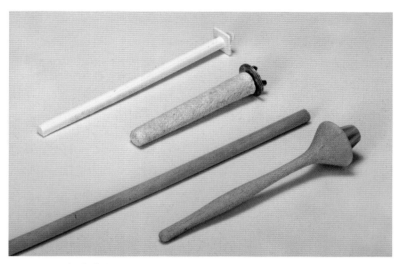

You may not find all the perches shown here in your local pet store, but do purchase perches in various sizes to give your budgie's feet exercise.

Water Tubes

YOU MAY FIND A CAGE EQUIPPED WITH WHAT IS KNOWN *as a sipper: a container for water with a stopper that holds a curved metal tube containing a ball bearing. The bird touches the tip of the tube with his tongue, which pushes back the ball bearing and allows a few drops of water to flow. Such sippers are widely used for small pet mammals, but they are not as commonly used for birds. Sippers must be located completely outside the cage, with only the end of the tube extending inside, or the budgie will chew through the rubber or plastic stopper. Sippers are easy to keep clean, since droppings and food crumbs cannot enter them, but they still need to be cleaned and refilled every day; you will also need to check each day to be sure your bird has not jammed the tip of the tube with a seed or other piece of food. If you try a sipper, be sure to also offer water in a cup each day, and pay attention to your bird's drinking patterns until you are certain he is drinking from the sipper.*

chance that droppings, food crumbs, or seed hulls will fall into the water—the perfect breeding ground for bacteria. Place cups where they are easily accessible for changing, cleaning, and refilling twice a day.

Perches

Some cages come equipped with one or two perches made of soft wood dowels of uniform size, roughly half an inch in diameter. There is nothing wrong with these perches, but budgies like a variety of perch sizes so they can stretch and relax the muscles and ligaments in their toes. Remove these dowels and offer your budgie at least three perches of varying diameters and materials.

Look for perches made of natural hardwoods, such as apple, manzanita, hazel, elm, or willow. These woods are harmless to budgies when chewed, and natural branches (which have been carefully sanitized and are not treated with preservatives or pesticides of any type) give a budgie a variety of diameters and shapes for comfortable perching. Your local pet store probably carries a variety of perches, and many online pet bird supply stores have a wide range as well.

You can make your own perches by cutting a length of branch and making slots in the ends to fit the bars of the cage. Be sure to correctly identify and select one of the safe woods mentioned above—never use conifers such as pine or yew, which can be toxic. Also avoid apricot, cherry, peach, prune, plum, and nectarine, which can be toxic as well. Soak the branch for an hour in a solution of 10 percent bleach and 90 percent water, rinse it thoroughly, and then soak it in clear water for three days, changing the water every twelve hours. Be sure there is *absolutely* no smell of chlorine from the perch and let it dry completely

This bathing cup has a convenient perch and enough room for the budgie to splash about—but any shallow container can make a good budgie bathtub.

before putting it in your budgie's cage. And never use bleach near your bird because even the fumes can be toxic.

Position the perches both high and low in the cage, and put one at an angle across a corner. Again, never put perches over or near food and water cups, and don't let them overlap if you have two budgies in a cage (the bird underneath will become covered with droppings during the night). Expect your budgie to chew up his perches on a regular basis, and be prepared to replace them as needed.

Some people use perches specially manufactured to control the growth of their budgies' nails. The idea is that a rough perch helps manicure the tips of the nails and keeps them from growing too long. Having one of these types of perches is fine, but be sure it isn't your budgie's only option in case it causes your budgie's feet discomfort. Avoid sandpaper covers for perches; they may cause raw, infected areas on the feet. Plan to trim your budgie's nails on a regular basis instead of trying to use a perch to do the job. (See chapter 7 for information on nail trimming.)

Bathing Supplies

Budgies love to splash around in shallow water. After getting totally wet, they preen, or groom, their feathers by running their beaks lengthwise down each feather and putting each barb back into place. At the same time, they spread a waterproofing oil from their preen (uropygial) glands over each feather.

Pet stores sell bathing cups for budgies and other small birds. These are shallow plastic cups with hoods designed to be placed in the cage for a few minutes a few times a week—or as often as the birds enjoy bathing. Put lukewarm water in the cup, put the cup in the cage, and let the budgie splash for a few minutes; then remove the cup, and let the budgie dry in a warm, draft-free area.

You may find that your budgie likes to bathe in his water cup, and this is perfectly okay as long as you check the cup a few times each day to be sure he hasn't splashed out all his drinking water. You can also offer your bird a shallow bowl or a plastic container similar to one you use for leftovers. Whatever you choose, be sure the container is shallow enough for your budgie to easily step up into and out of. You could also place your budgie under a trickling kitchen or bathroom faucet, but both of these rooms are often full of so many other dangers that it probably isn't worth the risk.

Some budgies ignore bathing dishes, but they will roll around in wet lettuce leaves. Try placing some on top of your budgie's cage at bath time.

Cage Cleaning Routines

You need to tend to the cage daily: twice a day (morning and early evening) to replace the food and water, and once to spot-clean the cage. Use a small cleaning brush or moist paper towel to remove droppings and loose feathers. (You will quickly discover that budgies are perpetually losing and replacing feathers during molting.) Remove and replace the paper on the cage bottom or tray. Clean all food and water cups with hot water and a drop of dishwashing liquid; rinse them thoroughly so no soap remains. You can wash your budgie's dishes in the dishwasher, but make sure there is no soap residue.

Every other day, clean the perches with a scrub brush dampened with warm water. Your local pet store carries scrub brushes that are specially made for cleaning the cage and perches. Every other week or so, remove the perches and give them a thorough cleaning. Scrub them with a bird-safe cleaning solution purchased from a pet store or from your veterinarian; then rinse and dry them. (Never use common household cleaners around your bird or on anything your bird may touch or chew. The likelihood of poisoning, either from ingestion or from fumes,

If your cage is too large for your kitchen sink, take it outdoors weekly and give it a thorough cleaning.

is very high.) If you have two sets of perches, place one set in the cage while you're cleaning the other.

Once a week, clean the entire cage by wiping down and scrubbing the bars, the tray, and the floor grate. Remove the majority of the debris with warm water and a scrub brush, and follow up with another round using a bird-safe cleaning solution on any tough spots. Finally, wipe down the cage with damp paper towels (or any clean, damp cloth) to remove any remaining cleaning solution. During this weekly cleaning, move your budgie to his travel cage or playgym so he isn't stressed.

Light and Dark

Do budgies need special lighting to be happy and healthy? The jury is still out, but budgies do seem to do best with some sunlight every day or so throughout the year. Budgies are diurnal birds in nature, which means they are active throughout the day (although they often rest in the shade when not feeding or flying). They certainly don't like continuous strong sunlight, which stresses them and may cause overheating. Never place a cage in or near a window where sunlight may stress the bird or drafts may form. You may bring your budgie's cage outside for a time on a sunny day, but always under supervision, and don't let the bird get overheated.

Several manufacturers sell special ultraviolet (UV) lights that can be placed over or near a budgie's cage and turned on for a few hours each day. These lights simulate the sun's ultraviolet rays and may help the budgie form or utilize certain vitamins. Natural UV light is blocked by window glass, so these lightbulbs are a much surer, safer way of providing light than putting the cage by a window.

Some budgies have trouble sleeping at night if the room isn't dark enough. A cover or blanket can help ensure that your budgie's nighttime slumber is undisturbed.

Budgies do need to sleep without disturbance for at least eight hours a night. In nature, budgies retreat to a protected roost as the sun goes down and tuck their heads under their feathers until the next sunrise, a period of roughly twelve hours. Put your budgie on a schedule; cover the cage with a lightweight but dark cover at perhaps eight o'clock in the evening, and let the bird sleep until the family gets up in the morning. The cover does not have to completely exclude light to work well, and it must not block all air movement into the cage.

Some budgies panic if they awake in total darkness and may hurt themselves by trying to escape their cages; their owners use small night-lights near the cages so the birds never have to sleep in total darkness. Most budgies, however, learn to sleep peacefully in their cages when the lights are turned off and the families leave them alone.

These little budgies appreciate the change of scene presented by this play cube. Variety is important for all parrots, so regularly change the toys you offer your budgie.

Toys, Toys, Toys

Budgies love toys, and toys are good for budgies. Parrots must be kept busy or they become withdrawn and morose; toys give them an outlet for their energy and something to do when their humans are not around or when their cage mates don't want to engage in mutual grooming. Never skimp on providing an array of suitable toys. Be sure to replace or rotate them regularly, and check them often to make sure they are still safe. (Ropes should not be dangerously frayed, the metal on chains should not be flaking off, and bell clappers should not be loose.)

Budgies prefer swings, mirrors, and bells as their basic toys, and they also love to go up and down ropes. All these toys are readily available in budgie-size versions at pet stores. There should be at least a swing and a bell in the cage waiting to greet the budgie when he first arrives in your home. The exact style of the toy is not that important, as long as it moves and maybe makes a little noise.

Be aware that not all toys are safe. Check for easily loosened clappers on bells, parts made of easily chewed toxic metals such as lead, and chrome plating that could peel off. Some plastic toys (unless they are made of a thick, hard plastic) are dangerous if chewed—which is certain to happen—as are any parts that are made of rubber.

Playgyms are activity areas that contain a variety of toys, including swings, ladders, and climbing ropes. In addition to the tabletop variety, there are treelike playgyms (also called play-stands) made from natural branches up to three feet high, with several cross branches from which you can hang toys. Many manufacturers offer a variety of styles made from interesting and attractive woods, including manzanita and sandblasted grape vines and roots. Make sure you purchase an appropriate-size playgym or cage-top platform; your budgie won't be able to navigate a playgym with perches that are too large or spaced too far apart, and he may be intimidated by bells and toys that are too big.

If you allow your budgie to play outside the cage on a playgym, you must supervise him at all times. Even if you keep

It's important to give your budgie out-of-cage time, but he won't be perfectly safe if his wing feathers aren't trimmed.

your budgie's wing feathers trimmed, he can quickly get into trouble or overestimate his flight powers. Playgyms should be placed only in rooms where no other pets are present—not even other free birds, who might attack a budgie—and certainly where there are no cats or dogs.

To Fly or Not to Fly

If you are interested in keeping budgies in an outdoor aviary rather than in indoor cages, keep in mind that birds kept outdoors are subject to storms and sudden cold snaps, as well as long periods of hot weather. They can even catch dangerous diseases from sparrows and pigeons who fly over their aviary and deposit contaminated droppings. Aviary budgies seldom become as bonded to their owners as do those kept indoors and given attention throughout the day.

Birds who never leave the aviary may never need their wing feathers trimmed. But if you keep your budgie indoors, you must decide whether or not to trim his wing feathers. Some people believe that a budgie with trimmed wing feathers will die of remorse from not being able to fly freely, but one hundred fifty years of domestic budgie ownership has proven this to be untrue. Fully flighted budgies tend to get into trouble when allowed out of their cages to explore a room, play on a playgym, or sit on your shoulder. They can fly into windows, toilets, and sinks; land on hot stoves; tempt dogs and cats; and escape—often never to be seen again—when a door or window is opened unexpectedly. Why risk these dangers? Play it safe, and trim his wing feathers. (See chapter 7 for information on trimming.)

5

The Proper Feeding of Budgies

This budgie seems to be truly relishing the meal! A proper diet is important for your budgie's health, but thankfully, it isn't difficult to provide.

IN NATURE, BUDGIES ARE GROUND FEEDERS WHO EAT THE small seeds of several Australian grasses; they rarely eat anything else unless desperate during droughts. Seeds provide wild budgies the high levels of fat they need to travel from place to place in search of water and food. Your pet budgie will prefer seeds over pelleted diets the same way a child may prefer french fries over a baked potato. If given in good variety along with a broad-based vitamin supplement, high-quality seeds could serve as a stable diet. However, the reality today is that seeds bought in stores are not always reliable foods; they may be old by the time you buy them, may be contaminated with insects and mold, and are not necessarily a complete food. Some seed mixes contain only the cheapest seeds, including red millet and even rice, which budgies seldom eat. Yes, your budgie could exist just on seeds, but she won't live as long or be as healthy as she could be.

Pelleted Diets

Start by feeding your budgie the diet she was getting in the pet store. If the store was offering only seed, then gradually introduce pellets. Each pellet has all the proteins, carbohydrates, fats, vitamins, and minerals required, eliminating the need for additional vitamins. Pelleted diets come in a great variety of sizes, shapes, and colors, and many mixtures are manufactured specifically for budgies. If your bird was not weaned onto a pelleted diet at the pet store, she may take a while to decide which colors or sizes she prefers; expect some waste for the first several weeks when you present the new food. Take the time to see what she likes, and never try to starve a bird into accepting a new food.

You should still provide high-quality seeds at each meal—about 50 percent of the total offered at first—and then gradually

Although pellets represent a large portion of your budgie's diet, seeds, along with fresh vegetables, should also be offered.

reduce the amount of seed over two to four weeks. Veterinarians recommend a diet that is 85 to 90 percent pellets and 10 to 15 percent seed and other treats (which can include healthy human foods such as vegetables and pasta). Ask your veterinarian about the proper proportions for your individual bird, based on her current weight and general health.

If you feed a diet of roughly 80 percent pellets (and your budgie actually eats the pellets), do not add vitamin supplements to the diet. This could lead to overdoses of several different vitamins, a condition, called hypervitaminosis, that could be dangerous or even fatal. Pelleted diets already have vitamins added and don't need extras. They also generally have enough calcium for all but laying hens.

Budgies will live well on just pellets, but they also seem to enjoy seeds as a form of entertainment. Some pellet manufacturers have begun including a healthful ratio of seeds in the same packages as their pelleted diets, providing just the right amount of fat and a bit of fun.

Greens, Vegetables, and Fruit

Your budgie will enjoy daily servings of greens and other vegetables. The simplest way to give greens is to hang a carrot top or a fresh leaf of spinach, kale, or dandelion from the top of the cage; you can use a special clip sold in stores or just a wooden clothespin (not plastic). If you mist the leaf before you place it in the cage, the budgie will be drawn to it both as food and as a source of water. If you prefer, you may tear up a leaf and add it to your budgie's normal food mix; just be sure to remove the leaf and replace the mix after just a few hours because the moisture from the leaf may cause bacteria to grow.

Some budgies enjoy fresh vegetables and fruit tidbits. Always keep in mind that some people foods are not healthy for budgies and that some can even cause them harm, so choose these items very carefully.

Some budgies will eat grated carrot, which is an excellent source of carotenes; carotenes will give your bird brighter yellow and green colors. You can also offer your budgie chopped bell peppers (from mild to spicy varieties), chunks of broccoli, and even very small amounts of cooked (and cooled) sweet potato. A piece of unsalted and unbuttered air-popped popcorn is another excellent low-fat treat, and it is something that many budgies seem to find very fun to nibble.

All About Seeds

The seeds usually offered to parrots fall into two broad groups: low fat and high fat. Both seeds should be included in a mix, although 75 percent of the mix should be low-fat seeds to prevent the budgie from becoming overweight. During the winter (if the budgie is kept outdoors) and during periods of

How Parrots Eat Seeds

ALL PARROTS HAVE VERY STRONG BEAKS. THEY USE these mighty beaks to open hard nuts and to hull their seeds before they are swallowed. As noted earlier, the tip of the budgie's lower beak is squared off and fits into a series of fine ridges under the tip of the upper beak. The tongue is a thick, specialized organ with small projections that allow it to hold an individual seed in position between the tip of the lower beak and the ridges of the upper. The tongue rolls the seed against the beak until one of the ridges makes a small break in the seed coating; further rolling strips the coat off the seed so the nutritious inner parts are exposed. The hull is spit out and the body of the seed is swallowed. This eliminates both the need for an extremely muscular crop and the need to swallow small mineral particles (often called grit) to hull the seed after it is swallowed.

Budgies hull their seeds individually, leaving a thick layer of empty hulls in their seed cups. One reason to feed your budgie twice a day is to remove the hulls so the bird can always reach fresh seeds.

stress—including mating and laying—a larger amount of high-fat seeds (commonly called oil seeds) can be given so the budgie has more energy and can store up some fat.

Low-Fat (Starchy) Seeds

In low-fat seeds, most of the nutrition comes from carbohydrates (starches and sugars), which may make up 55 to 65 percent of the weight. Another 10 to 15 percent comes from proteins, with just 4 to 10 percent coming from fats. Low-fat seeds have good levels of fat-soluble vitamin E plus generally high levels of the water-soluble B vitamin complex. They also have adequate amounts of calcium and other minerals.

This budgie is happily nibbling on a millet spray. These sprays are popular treats that can easily be clipped to the side of the cage for a convenient snack.

- Canary Seed: This little pale brown seed generally forms the basis of many budgie mixes, along with millets. Although it takes many canary seeds to make a meal, they are nutritionally excellent.

- Oats: Familiar as a grain used in many human cereals and breads, oats are an important budgie food as well. Although relatively inexpensive, oats are nutritious and easily digested. All mixes containing oats (especially the prehulled seeds known as groats) must be kept dry and tightly closed, or they will go bad by absorbing moisture from the air.

- Millets: Many different types of millets are grown around the world for animal foods (as sorghum); but those generally found in the better budgie mixes are the small, round, white types often called proso and pearl millets. The coarse red millets apparently taste bad to many birds and are simply rejected, so any mixes with obviously large amounts of red millet are not good buys. Millet sprays are one of a budgie's favorite foods and can be given as treats in half-inch lengths (great as rewards during training) or hung from a convenient and clean spot in the cage for a late-day snack. Try not to give too many sprays, however, as eventually they are turned to fat, and your bird may come to prefer them over better, more varied foods.

High-Fat (Oily) Seeds

High-fat seeds, which may be quite large, are excellent for growing birds and ill birds, but they contain too much fat to be used as more than a small percentage of the entire mix. These seeds may consist of 40 percent fat or more, with lots of protein and very few carbohydrates. Owners of outdoor birds may feed fatty seeds often during the winter—when they are needed to provide quick metabolic heat—and in small quantities during the summer.

• Sunflower Seeds: You can harvest sunflower seeds from flowers raised in your own garden, but you will need lots of plants and will end up with only a few seeds because they are picked by wild birds and squirrels before they ripen. Budgies will hull sunflower seeds, but they much prefer to feed on the hulled hearts or chips, leading quickly to weight gain. Sunflower seeds contain roughly 45 percent oils and 25 percent proteins, with only a small amount of starch, so they are good for stressful situations and are often given to laying females and to budgies kept outdoors during winter. Because hearts are easy to digest and a good source of energy, they are commonly fed to sick birds.

- Niger: These slender black seeds are about the size of canary seed, but they contain a large amount of oil (roughly 40 percent) and about 20 percent proteins; they are a good but a fattening food. Yes, a budgie can and will hull such tiny seeds. This is one of the most expensive seeds when purchased alone. Keep any mix with niger dry and in the dark to prevent the seeds from becoming rancid.

- Flax: Also called linseed (and the source of linseed oil), flax seeds come from a plant that produces bright blue flowers and a fibrous stem used to manufacture linen cloth. The seeds are tiny but high in oil. Many budgies do not like flax seeds and reject them from a mix.

- Rape Seed: These tiny seeds also are high in oil, but you seldom find them in American budgie mixes. Rape is a type of commercially grown mustard that is important for feeding crops in some areas of Europe. These seeds are also a good source of minerals, and they contain about 50 percent fats.

Common seed mixes for budgies contain mostly canary seeds, proso millet, oat groats, and some sunflower chips, providing a good group of seeds at a reasonable price. When supplemented with a millet or foxtail spray and perhaps a few extra sunflower seeds, these mixes give your budgie a good variety. However, if you feed only seeds (which is strongly discouraged by most avian veterinarians), consider adding a good brand of vitamin supplement to the mix once a week. Just keep in mind that giving your bird too many additional vitamins is as dangerous as or more so than giving her too few, so consult with your veterinarian.

Like all parrots, budgies have specialized beaks and tongues that allow them to fully hull each seed before ingesting it.

People Food

Your budgie will think of herself as part of the family and may want to try the things you eat. In many cases, this may not be safe or nutritious. Some foods that are safe for us are toxic to birds. Budgies can't digest many of the things we eat, and the salt, sugar, and fat found in many of our foods (especially processed foods) would be especially unhealthy to a budgie. One exception is cooked noodles of various types, which are often included in commercial bird food mixes that are designed to be cooked before being fed to a budgie. Offer them in only small amounts. There is no reason to offer your budgie meat, chicken, fish, or insects.

European budgie owners often supplement the diet of laying hens with such things as wheat bread soaked in milk (for extra calcium), boiled eggs (also given to young budgies), and yogurt. Budgies cannot digest milk, which causes diarrhea. Yogurt can be used as a dietary supplement in very small amounts, however, as can finely chopped boiled egg. All these foods spoil quickly, so never mix them with seeds, or you will have to throw everything away in a few hours. Yogurt with active bacterial cultures, by the way, can be given to a budgie who has been on antibiotics; it helps regenerate the useful bacteria in the gut.

Does a Budgie Need Grit?

Grit is a finely ground calcium-rich material often derived from oyster shells or limestone rocks. It is meant to serve both as a source of calcium and to help grind tough seeds in the gizzard of a bird (specifically, a chicken). Budgies and other parrots, however, hull their seeds before swallowing them, so there is no need for

Fruits and vegetables are great for budgies, and this fellow is enjoying the variety in his diet. But many people foods are simply not healthy for birds, so choose wisely.

Foods to Avoid

SOME FOODS ARE SIMPLY NOT SAFE TO FEED TO BUDGIES. *One of the worst is unsweetened chocolate; it contains high levels of the chemical theobromine, which can cause death in a small bird. Avoid milk chocolate as well. Avocado pits contain a toxin, persin, that can cause death even in very small amounts. Sometimes the toxin leaks from the pit into the flesh next to it, making the whole fruit dangerous. To be safe, avoid avocado in all its forms and fruit pits of any type. Salty and sweet foods should also be avoided, along with wildflowers and most flowers from the garden. Fertilizers and insecticides should not be used near any plants that will be fed to budgies.*

having grit in the gizzard to grind the seeds. Giving grit to a young budgie can cause death if the bird eats too much and the grit stops up her crop. Today, the general advice is to not give grit to budgies.

This is a typical cuttlebone from a pet store, complete with metal hanger and ready to be clipped to the side of the cage.

This doesn't mean, however, that you can't give calcium and mineral supplements to your bird. Mineral blocks are widely sold in pet stores; at worst they seem harmless, and they might actually be of use for some birds. Many owners offer cuttlebones to their birds, especially laying females. Cuttlebones are the internal shells of a type of squid, and they are rich in calcium and other minerals. They also are heavy in salt, but the salt in a cuttlebone seems to do little harm. If you worry about salt, cut the shell into quarters to expose the soft material under the hard outer skin. Peel off the skin (a knife blade works well), and then soak the soft part of the shell in very hot water for a few minutes. (Don't soak it so long that mold could develop, of course.) Then dry it and either offer it in a holder or grind it up and add it to the seed mix.

Feeding Routines

Feed your budgie twice a day, early in the morning and early in the evening, in line with a budgie's natural feeding behaviors. The early evening feeding should be larger than the morning feeding, but typically a teaspoon of food will suffice. After an hour, check to see what has been eaten, and scoop off any seed hulls with a small spoon. Leave some food and a millet spray in the cage at night in case your budgie wakes and wants to feed a bit.

Offer fresh water when you offer the food. Generally speaking, if your home's water supply is safe for you, it is safe for your budgie. Still, some budgie owners feel more comfortable offering their birds bottled water or water that is filtered at the tap.

Don't overfeed your budgie, and don't make rapid changes in her diet. Budgies like routines and prefer that things stay the same; they don't adjust well to change. If you must make changes to her diet, do it gradually.

Always use the best mixes and foods you can find to have a happy, healthy budgie.

6

Training Your Budgie

This owner and pet have clearly established a bond of trust and affection. This bond is essential if you plan to handle and train your budgie, but an untrained budgie can still be a delightful pet.

THE BEST BUDGIES TO TRAIN ARE YOUNG BIRDS WHO have established strong bonds with their owners—or at least with humans in general. An adult budgie who has not bonded with you or with any other human will be more difficult to train and perhaps cannot be trained at all. He can still be a wonderful pet if all you are looking for is a happy, whistling, chattering bird to keep you company and to entertain you simply by doing what budgies do; he just won't be a bird you can handle. This is one reason that hand-fed and hand-reared budgies (as well as other parrots) command higher prices than do those raised by their parents. They learn to trust humans by constantly being handled when taken out to be fed, and they learn to associate people with the comfort of being touched and of having full bellies.

The first step in training is to establish trust, which is created through frequent positive interaction. Once your budgie has your trust, he will have the confidence to accept your direction.

Young birds who are still bonding to you do best when kept out of contact with other budgies, who might distract them. Trained budgies can quickly lose their training if placed into a large cage with several untrained budgies, as they revert to bonding with other budgies. Your bird will need several weeks of handling to form a strong attachment, so if you want two birds, wait at least two or three months before you purchase the second budgie. And note that although a male will probably retain his bond with you even while courting and mating, a female will most likely lose her training during the time she is incubating her eggs and taking care of her young.

Basic Training

All budgies should be taught to step up onto your hand or finger, step onto a perch of any length, and accept being wrapped in a towel. The first skill is referred to as finger training, or hand training; the second as perch training; and the last as towel training. These three simple maneuvers, which can be taught with persistence and gentleness, are all your budgie really needs to know to be a great pet.

Finger Training

The first things to teach your budgie are to hop up onto your outstretched finger or hand while in his cage, to leave the cage on your hand, and to hop back down into the cage when returned. To begin, you have to form your first strong bonds with your budgie and earn his trust.

Start the training two or three days after the bird arrives in your home and becomes used to his new cage and surroundings. Approach the cage and talk gently to the bird. Occasionally, offer a small bit of foxtail millet as a treat or incentive for good behavior. Give your bird this attention for a minute or two each hour, several hours a day, for the first three or four days. By then, you should have a relaxed bird who knows you and expects you to offer food and attention. Most budgies adjust rapidly, and their owners gain their confidence in just a day or two. When you

Like this budgie, your bird should quickly learn to step up onto your finger while inside the cage and out.

think you are gaining your budgie's confidence, lightly pet the top of his head or around the nape of his neck. Never tire the bird out by petting him after he has lost interest; let him relax, and then start again in an hour or later that day.

The next training step is to reach into the cage with your index finger extended. The bird should be interested, and he should hop over for petting. Move your finger under the bird where he can hop on, and firmly give the command *step up* so the budgie associates the sound with the action. Practice this basic training up to ten minutes at a time, several times a day. Within a few days, the budgie should become accustomed to your finger and hop up immediately when you give the command.

Once you are sure the bird understands the command, take him out of the cage while on your finger or hand. (This is one reason you want a cage with a large door.) The bird may be frightened at first, so don't push him too strongly. Most budgies will want to get out and explore, so they may be eager to leave their cages. If your budgie's wing feathers are trimmed, he won't be able to fly around the room (although he may startle and fly to the floor); but if his wings are untrimmed, make sure you practice this step in a closed room. Any trip outside the cage can be dangerous, so make sure the room in which you train is safe; check electrical outlets and cords, remove possible high perching spots, and don't let any other pets into the room.

Even with time and patience, some budgies may be hesitant to accept strange hands entering their cages and will not be receptive to finger training. Your budgie may even nip at your finger. In this case, your budgie is more likely to step up onto your finger if you first allow him to come out and climb onto the cage top or onto a perch attached to the outside of the cage.

Once your budgie understands the *step up* and *off* commands, teach him to step up onto a perch and down (off) onto your finger or hand.

Another way to reduce the chance of territorial biting is to practice training in a "neutral" territory, such as on a playgym in a room away from the cage. If your bird is still nippy, a final option is to begin step up training with a perch (discussed in the next section) and then work up to using your finger.

Once you and your budgie have mastered the *step up* command, teach the bird to step back off your hand or finger when he is returned to the cage. Use a simple command such as *step down*, or *off*, and gently maneuver the bird back onto the floor of his cage or onto a favorite perch. Repeat this process until the bird understands what you want and feels secure responding to the command.

Different budgies learn at different rates; some simply adjust better than others do. Never get angry or frustrated with a slow learner. Always be gentle and patient, and keep repeating the training session for short intervals several times a day. Eventually the budgie will associate the command with the action. Keep refreshing the training by repeating the sequence every day. Budgies can forget their training if placed in their cages and not asked to practice their new skills.

Perch Training

Next you want to get the bird used to stepping onto a perch. Start with a short perch, eventually working up to a perch that is maybe two to four feet long. This training will allow you to retrieve a frightened bird from a shelf, light fixture, or other position high up in a room or—in the worst case—from a low branch on a tree outdoors.

Using a short perch, repeat the basic training steps for teaching the bird to climb on and off your finger. Use the same

This budgie has learned to accept being wrapped in a towel. It takes some patience to towel train your pet bird, but the training will make your bird much easier to handle when ill or injured.

simple commands so the budgie doesn't really have to learn anything new. Keep training simple and fun, and give an occasional treat to keep the bird interested. You will be able to tell when the bird becomes tired and just won't learn any more during a session, so let him relax and try again in an hour or two. Eventually, almost all budgies learn to step up onto a perch.

Towel Training

You or your veterinarian may need to handle your budgie when he is sick or injured. An injured or scared budgie is panicky and will not respond to simple commands. If you try to hold a squirming bird with a glove, he is likely to bite you, and he may learn to distrust your hand. And veterinarians do not enjoy trying to examine or treat birds, even small budgies, who are constantly trying to bite and scratch them. The best bet is to teach your budgie to actually enjoy being wrapped in a towel and be willing to extend just a wing or a foot for simple treatments such as wing and nail trimming. Toweling him gives you control of the bird and reduces the risk of further injury.

Make this training time enjoyable for the bird. Place a towel on a tabletop or other stable surface, and put a treat or toy in the center (such as a piece of millet spray, a bit of apple, a raisin, or a favorite bell). Allow the budgie to walk over to the treat, and then spend a few minutes interacting with him. Once the bird has become comfortable spending some time on the towel, slowly pull one corner toward (and eventually over) the bird while speaking gently to him and petting him. You may need to repeat this several times because budgies are easily frightened by objects approaching them from above; but with persistence, you can teach yours to accept being covered.

Some budgies enjoy having their bellies petted. Your bird may not be comfortable in the belly-up position, however, so don't push him if he repeatedly resists the training.

Once your bird is used to having one corner pulled up, proceed to a second corner and then a third, finally closing the entire towel loosely over the bird (and his treat). Ultimately, you want be able to lift your budgie and hold him firmly but gently while he is in the towel. You may find that your bird will more readily accept being wrapped in a brightly colored towel than in a dark or white one, and your bird may prefer a smooth material to terrycloth, which can get caught on his nails.

Can Your Budgie Speak?

Budgies are as intelligent as many larger parrots, and they have the same type of tongue and sound box (the syrinx, which contains the equivalent of vocal cords). Their small size, however, means that any words they repeat will be very high pitched—often close to squeaks—and the words may be hard to distinguish from whistles. Budgies can repeat words and other sounds, but you may have to listen very closely to tell just what sounds they

Belly Up

MOST PARROTS CAN BE TRAINED TO LIE ON THEIR BACKS in their owners' hands. It's a cute trick, and it is a position that veterinarians can use to examine the birds. Training is done by slowly and repeatedly tipping the bird back into the cupped palm of one hand while he is perched on the other. You can also train your budgie to perch on your thumb; then wrap your hand around his body and tip him back. Unfortunately, many budgies are too excitable to accept this position and never will allow you to hold them with the belly up. You can try to teach your pet this position, but don't expect too much.

are repeating. Don't expect your budgie to ever sound as clear as an African grey or an Amazon parrot, whose larger sound boxes produce more modulated tones that can actually resemble human intonation.

Not all budgies will learn to speak. Males are more likely to speak than females are; they also tend to have louder and clearer voices and are less likely to forget their training. Females often become more involved with laying eggs than with speaking, but many female budgies do learn to speak and are quite understandable. But there are exceptions to every rule, and many budgie owners would disagree with these gender-based observations.

When it is time for a speech-training session, move your budgie's cage to a place where he cannot hear other budgies or other birds and where he will not be distracted by a TV, radio, or stereo. Or move just your budgie into another room, placing him on a playgym or into his travel cage or keeping him perched on your finger. You want him to be able to concentrate only on you and the many repetitions necessary to learn to speak.

Teaching a budgie to talk takes a lot of time and patience—and repetition. This bird is listening attentively: an essential ingredient for success.

Get close to your budgie, and make sure you have his attention; having him perched on your finger is a great way to show him it is time to focus. Begin with a simple word of one or two hard syllables—teaching him his own name is a great way to start. Repeat the word slowly and distinctly. Use a constant cadence, and say the word exactly the same way each time. Start with a ten-minute session several times a day, and eventually move to sessions up to twenty minutes long. You will be able to tell when your bird becomes bored and wants to play, but don't give up too quickly at each session.

How long will it take to teach the first word? It may take two or three days, or it could take a week. Or, as mentioned earlier, your budgie may never learn to speak.

Once your budgie has learned his name, move on to a second word that sounds quite different but still has only one or

Use a Recording

TEACHING A BUDGIE TO SPEAK CAN BE A LONG, SLOW process, but many companies have produced teaching aids to make your job easier. Any pet store that sells birds or bird supplies is certain to have one or two training tapes or CDs. Some aids are excellent and well planned, and others are a bit skimpier in presentation, but any may still help just by exposing your bird to constant repetition. However, many experienced bird owners believe there is no substitute for the one-on-one training time you spend with your bird. Consider training tapes and CDs a supplement to your budgie's training, not the main means.

two syllables. Keep repeating until the bird learns the word. Once your bird has learned two words, continue to expand his vocabulary as much as possible. Many budgies learn their names and little else, whereas some learn two or three dozen words.

Other Tricks

Their small size prevents budgies from performing many physical tricks common to other parrots, such as roller-skating or skateboarding, but they have a good sense of balance and can learn to walk a tightrope, flip objects out of a spoon, ring a bell, and engage in other similar activities. Many pet stores sell books with suggestions and methods for simple tricks that can be taught to budgies, and some birds seem to enjoy learning to perform with their owners.

Here is one very simple "trick": offer your budgie a small wad of paper. His first instinct, after juggling it around with his beak, will be to toss it to the floor. Each time your budgie sees you pick it up and hand it back to him, he begins to understand

Your budgie may never learn any fancy tricks, but even climbing a ladder, as these two are, is entertaining for you to watch and good exercise for your bird.

the cause and effect—and he enjoys it! If you place a large hoop of brightly colored plastic at the edge of the table where your budgie normally throws the paper, he will throw the paper through the hoop. With repetition (and a few treats), you can train your budgie to consistently throw the paper through smaller and smaller hoops at different heights. You can also switch to using a small, plastic Wiffle ball (available at most pet super-stores). Eventually, you can teach your budgie to play a little game of basketball with you.

Sometimes, budgies teach what they have learned to their pals and cage mates.

7

Keeping Your Budgie Healthy

Your budgies will depend on you to keep them healthy. In addition to giving them healthful diets, take them to the veterinarian for regular checkups.

ALTHOUGH BUDGIES ARE VERY HARDY BIRDS, THEY ARE subject to a variety of bacterial and viral illnesses. They may have genetic medical conditions, or they may be exposed to disease through interactions with other birds. Your budgie can develop nutritional deficiencies and metabolic problems if she is kept on a poor seed-only diet instead of on a pelleted diet that contains the range of vitamins she needs. If she is fed too much food and doesn't get a chance to exercise several times each day, she will become overweight, storing fat both under the skin and around her internal organs.

Although you will be able to control what your budgie eats and limit her exposure to birds who may be carrying disease, there are many illnesses beyond your control. And you may not

Your first job as a pet owner is to make sure you select a healthy bird from the breeder or pet store. You can check for obvious signs of illness or injury, but have a veterinarian examine the bird as well. If the bird is ill, return her for a refund or exchange.

be able to recognize these conditions without the guidance of a veterinarian trained to care for parrots.

First Things First

Choose a local veterinarian experienced with birds before you bring your budgie home. Plan to schedule an appointment for your bird's first examination to occur as early as the day you purchase her, and certainly no more than three days after. This exam will confirm that you have purchased a healthy bird, and it is likely to be required by your pet store's written health guarantee. Any reputable pet store offers a written guarantee of some type, generally stating that, if within a certain number of days (usually anywhere from three to thirty days) a veterinarian determines the bird is ill, the store will replace the bird or refund the cost.

Because birds are so adept at hiding illness and only a qualified veterinarian can recognize many common problems, a pet store may mistakenly sell a sick bird now and then. Always ask the pet store about its guarantee process, and get it in writing.

Finding a Veterinarian

Many veterinarians have some experience with birds, but you should try to find one who is certified in avian practice by the American Board of Veterinary Practitioners (ABVP). These veterinarians have the title Diplomate ABVP—Avian Practice listed after their names, or they are described as board-certified avian veterinarians. You can locate one of these highly qualified avian veterinarians either by calling the ABVP at 800-697-3583 or by using the search tool on the ABVP Web site: go to http://www.abvp.com/finddiplomate.aspx, and enter your city and state.

The requirements for ABVP certification and recertification are demanding, so there are only about one hundred veterinarians certified in avian practice. It may be difficult to find one in your area. In this case, select a member of the Association of Avian Veterinarians (AAV). Membership in this organization is a strong indicator of both a veterinarian's experience with birds and his or her interest in staying up to date on avian medicine. There are about three thousand members of the AAV worldwide, and they can be located through the AAV Web site at http://www.aav.org. Enter your city, state, zip code, or area code into the search tool at http://aav.org/vet-lookup, or call 817-428-7900.

Another source for recommendations is the pet store where you purchased your budgie. Any reputable pet store will have one or more avian veterinarians on call, and they will probably know about other local veterinarians simply from talking with their customers. If your pet store sells *Bird Talk* magazine, it

will either have on hand or will be able to order you a copy of an
annual magazine called *BIRDS USA* (http://www.birdsusa.com)

Crossing Borders

WHEN BIRDS ARE IMPORTED FROM ANOTHER COUNTRY,
they are required to undergo a period of isolation called quaran-
tine. During this time—commonly forty-five to sixty days—the
birds are closely observed for signs of several contagious
diseases and are given tests to see if they are carrying
psittacosis or other dangerous illnesses. Budgies sold in local
pet stores are most likely bred in the United States, so quaran-
tine is unnecessary.

Many budgies cross state borders, and import laws vary
widely from state to state. Some states require a veterinary
health certificate or a minimal quarantine period to observe the
birds for symptoms of diseases that could spread to other birds,
especially poultry. Outbreaks of poultry diseases can cost mil-
lions of dollars. If your bird was brought in from another state,
there may be legal paperwork that should accompany her at the
time of sale. Ask the store if your bird was bred locally or came
from a breeder in another state.

It is almost impossible to carry a budgie legally across
international borders. You might be able to carry your budgie
into Mexico, but to get it back into the United States would
mean paperwork, a period of quarantine, and high legal and
care costs; the same applies to traveling to Canada. And remem-
ber that your budgie could easily pick up contagious diseases
when transported into a new area.

If you are moving from one state to another, you may need
to show your bird's health certificate to legally cross the state
line. For a small fee, a veterinarian can provide you with a
health certificate that is valid for a short period of time to cover
your move. Make sure to have a new veterinarian awaiting you
when you get to your new home, in case the stress of traveling
makes your bird ill.

This well-trained bird is ready for an examination. Be sure you select a qualified avian vet before you purchase your bird, and take her in for her first checkup right away.

that publishes a very thorough directory of avian veterinarians.

Once you have found a few veterinarians to interview, don't be afraid to ask questions about their educational backgrounds and professional experience. Veterinarians who love what they do are happy to talk about their qualifications; and if they love what they do, it is a positive sign about the quality of care they will provide your budgie.

Your Budgie's First Exam

Your budgie's recorded medical history starts with the first checkup by a veterinarian. A bird's metabolism is very high compared with a human's (the normal body temperature commonly is over 102 degrees Fahrenheit and the heart beats more than 200 times a minute), and parrots as small as budgies can become ill quickly, develop few symptoms, and die before it is possible for a veterinarian to provide treatment. For this reason, your veterinarian will take blood samples during the first office visit, subject the samples to a variety of blood chemistry tests, and use this information to develop a baseline record of how your budgie's body chemistry works when she is well. This record makes it easier and faster to recognize problems that occur later.

Blood chemistry also allows your veterinarian to detect whether the budgie is suffering from diabetes, has liver or kidney problems, and has certain types of cancers. Blood tests can identify the presence of a variety of dangerous illnesses, including bacteria and viruses the bird might be carrying without developing the disease itself. If your budgie is an asymptomatic carrier of certain diseases, she could spread the illness to other parrots (not just budgies) just by being present in the same room; some of these diseases are deadly.

In addition to taking blood samples, your veterinarian will conduct a complete physical examination of the budgie. This includes checking the eyes, mouth, nostrils, ears, legs, toes, and

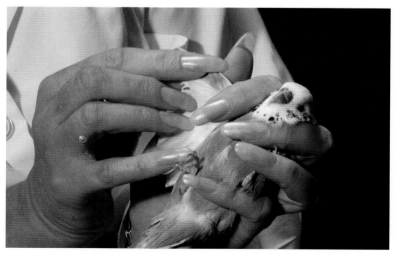

Part of a regular veterinary exam is a complete physical inspection of the bird, including the wings and feathers.

wings as well as looking at general feather texture and development. The vet will check the throat and crop for tumors and crop impactions (most likely in young birds). The vent and the feathers around it will be examined carefully for signs of diarrhea (such as dirty feathers), unusual swellings, or evidence of bleeding. The uropygial gland over the base of the tail (the one that provides the oil the bird uses when preening) will be checked for tumors, which are not uncommon in larger parrots and are sometimes found in budgies.

The veterinarian will weigh your budgie and take note of how much fat is present under the skin of the chest. Obesity is a common problem in budgies and can lead to a number of diseases, so it is important to have this baseline measurement to later determine whether your budgie has become overweight. A young budgie often still has a layer of "baby fat" under the skin that will burn off in a few months. In an older budgie, excess fat may indicate that the bird has long been on a poor diet or has not had enough exercise (both easy problems to correct); but extra fat can also indicate a more serious problem. An adult budgie's weight should stay approximately the same—roughly an ounce or two (more for the largest English budgies)—throughout her life. For an accurate measurement, birds are commonly weighed in grams; twenty-five to thirty-five grams is an acceptable range for an American budgie.

The veterinarian will also take a fecal sample (usually by passing a swab inside the vent as well as collecting fresh droppings) and check it for parasites. The sample is suspended in a high-density chemical solution that forces the eggs of tapeworms, flukes, and roundworms—as well as cysts of some protozoans and other parasites—to float to the surface. Then they are placed on

Your veterinarian will be able to determine the sex of your budgie, either through a blood test or by visual examination. This normal green budgie has a solid yellow head (no banding) and a blue cere, indicating he is an adult male.

a slide and examined under a microscope to identify and count them. Many vets send fecal samples to outside labs to be checked in more detail than is possible during the office visit. Serious parasitic infestations will be treated at the time of the exam.

The veterinarian can also confirm the sex of your young budgie through a simple blood or feather test (which is sent out to a special lab). In many cases, the veterinarian will be able to tell the sex of your budgie, once she is about four months old, by the color of the cere; but with some color mutations, the cere color does not indicate sex, and so a blood test is needed.

Yearly Exams

In nature, a sick bird is the first to be noticed by a predator and killed. For this reason, birds have adapted to show no signs of illness until their final days, or hours, are near. This is why you must take your budgie to the veterinarian for a checkup each year. During the checkup, the veterinarian will repeat much of what was done during the initial exam, including checking your budgie's general condition, performing a fecal examination for

Good Budgie!

NO VETERINARIAN WANTS TO EXAMINE A SCREAMING bird, and veterinarians certainly don't like being bitten, even by a small budgie who can barely draw blood. Your veterinarian will know how to handle your budgie and may use a towel for easy handling. Many breeders train a young bird to accept being wrapped in a towel just for this reason; check to see if your new bird has already been towel trained. If not, you can train her yourself. (See chapter 6 for information on towel training.)

This cooperative budgie has accepted being wrapped in a towel and is calmly extending a foot, ready for a nail trimming.

intestinal parasites, and taking blood for any necessary blood work. (Most veterinarians recommend a full blood workup every one to three years.) Your veterinarian will also weigh your bird and discuss any changes that may be needed in your budgie's diet.

This is an excellent time to have the veterinarian check to see if the wing feathers need to be trimmed again. New wing feathers come in over a period of several weeks during the molt, not all at once; some new feathers can come in as often as every six months, and if you fail to detect that your bird is now flighted, she could escape.

Veterinary Costs

Your budgie will live about five to eight years on average, but she could live as long as fifteen years with the right diet and regular veterinary care. If your budget is tight, don't be embarrassed to ask the veterinarian for an estimate of the cost of the exam first;

Birds are notoriously good at hiding illnesses. Closely watch for any changes in your bird's eating habits or general behavior that may signal a medical problem.

you may be able to establish a payment plan. Each individual test done on a blood sample or sent to an outside lab has a price, so a full battery of tests can get expensive. To perform DNA tests on blood samples (sometimes necessary to determine the sex of color mutations who don't have obvious external differences) could cost twenty dollars or more per test. Although most veterinarians won't run unnecessary tests, you can still expect to spend from one hundred to three hundred dollars for each office visit—sometimes more if several lab tests are necessary.

Emergencies

Keep a close eye on your bird's behavior and appearance, and note any changes, no matter how small. If your bird becomes quieter or noisier than usual, is more or less affectionate, ignores a favorite toy or snack, or stops drinking, consult your veterinarian immediately. There may be nothing wrong (although failure to drink is usually a sign of a serious problem), but it is better to

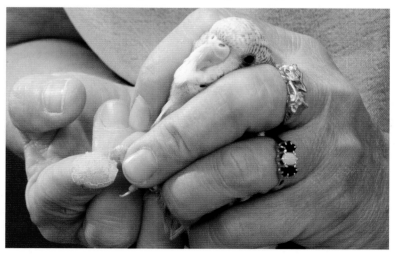

Always keep styptic powder or cornstarch on hand for small bleeding problems. Hold your bird firmly but gently, and apply the powder liberally to the wound.

Bleeding

BLEEDING IS PROBABLY THE MOST COMMON EMERGENCY situation in budgies. An actively growing blood feather can rupture, leading to bleeding on or under the skin. Sometimes a budgie catches a toe or nail in the cage bars or on a toy and pulls off the nail. If not treated, both problems can lead to serious blood loss. Styptic powder, sold in pet stores, will stop most minor bleeding. If that isn't available, try dabbing cornstarch or flour on the bleeding spot to help it clot. Head for the veterinarian immediately if clotting doesn't occur within a minute or so.

make a phone call and at least talk to the veterinarian than to let a serious problem develop. Many illnesses can be fatal in one or two days from the time obvious signs first appear.

For minor colds and other respiratory problems, you can take temporary measures the moment you notice sneezing or a runny nostril. Keep the bird warmer than usual, and move her to a smaller cage with just one perch set low near the cage bottom. You may want to move the budgie to a bathroom and run a hot shower to keep the room warm and moist. When you transport your sick budgie to the veterinarian, make sure that she can stay warm, is not subjected to any drafts, and is kept in a darkened or covered travel cage (preferably) to help keep her calm.

Trimming Wing Feathers

As mentioned earlier, the decision to trim the wing feathers of a budgie is a personal one. Trimming the wing feathers makes sense if you often allow your pet to roam about on your shoulder, explore the outside of her cage, or spend time on a playgym. (All these activities provide exercise and enrichment, so they *should*

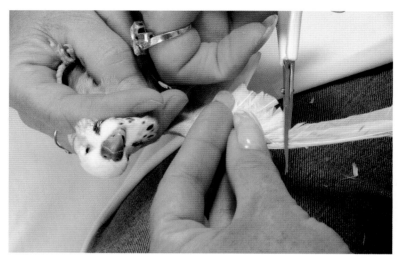

Here the bird's primary flight feathers are being trimmed. Be sure to have someone experienced show you how to trim the feathers, and always trim the feathers of both wings.

be part of your budgie's daily routine.) Any bird can become excited and haphazardly take flight in a panic, injuring or killing herself by flying at full speed into a window, mirror, or wall—or escaping out an open window or door. Trimming the wing feathers doesn't hurt the bird, and the procedure is not difficult to do once you've learned how. Some owners let their veterinarian do the trimming at the yearly exam, but this won't be frequent enough to keep your bird safe. Remember that wing feathers are replaced over an interval of several weeks and certainly more than once during the course of a calendar year. If you don't pay attention to the condition of the wing feathers, your supposedly trimmed bird could fly away when you least expect it. Trimming is a grooming chore you'll want to be able to do yourself.

Trimming your budgie's wing feathers is just like cutting your own hair. No bones or muscles are cut—just feathers, which grow back. Have a veterinarian or bird breeder show you how to

This is a blood feather, and you can see how it got its name. Once the feather is fully formed, it no longer has a supply of blood and can safely be trimmed.

do it the first time so you know which feathers to cut and which to avoid. You should never trim a blood feather; blood feathers are new feathers just starting to emerge from their protective sheaths under the skin of the wing. They are liberally supplied with blood during this stage of growth, and cutting them could lead to serious blood loss. Keep styptic powder or cornstarch on hand in case you accidentally trim a blood feather, and be prepared to take your budgie to the veterinarian if the bleeding doesn't stop.

There are several ways to trim wing feathers, but the safest technique involves cutting the first five to eight primary feathers—the long flight feathers. A strong budgie may need to have eight feathers cut, whereas a weak budgie may need only five trimmed. Start with five, and let your bird take off from your hand from about a foot off the floor. If the bird quickly gains altitude instead of gliding to the ground, trim one more feather on

These nails are healthy and nicely formed. To keep them that way, be sure to trim your budgie's nails (or have a vet trim them) frequently: they grow quickly!

each side, and try again. You want her to be able to gain some altitude to prevent crash landings, but a budgie shouldn't be able to fly more than a couple of feet into the air.

In the past, some pet bird owners trimmed just one set of wing feathers, but this left the bird off balance and resulted in uneven flight and uncontrolled landings (and injury!). Trim the same number of feathers from both wings.

Keeping your budgie's wing feathers trimmed is a year-round job. Caged budgies in the United States generally molt in the late spring, but the process can happen at almost any time of the year, depending on light, temperature, diet, general health, and age. Typically, an old primary feather at about the middle of each wing is shed first, and then other primaries are shed in an alternating fashion on either side of the middle primary; at no time are all the primaries gone. Budgies are relatively quick molters, but the process may take several weeks for the wings and tail. Remember that all the feathers of the body are molted at some point during the year, which explains the constant presence of one or two little body feathers on the cage floor.

Trimming the Nails

Your budgie's nails will grow quickly and can become twisted if not trimmed. Twisted nails easily catch in the bars of the cage or even on your clothing, and a long nail can be broken or pulled out and bleed. Your veterinarian can show you how to trim the nails, which is much like trimming the nails of a dog or cat. Just remember that the base of the nail (called the quick) is supplied with blood and must not be cut. You will typically need to trim the nails every two or three months, although diets high in protein cause faster nail (and feather) growth. Use a pair of small clipping scissors designed for pets (available through your veterinarian or a pet store) or a small set of human nail clippers. (The more com-

Overgrown Beaks

AN OVERGROWN BEAK CAN MAKE IT DIFFICULT FOR A budgie to hull seeds and can lead to starvation. Occasionally, the beak develops irregular edges, or the top and bottom become out of line with each other as a result of uneven growth, parasite infestation (mites can live in the tissues at the base of the beak), or an accident. Because the beak is made of secreted substances and is not truly living, your veterinarian can trim it back to the proper shape by using fine scissors or a small rotary tool with sanding drums. Beak trims are strictly a job for your veterinarian, however; it is easy to misjudge and overtrim the beak. Your veterinarian will examine your budgie's beak as part of a normal checkup or when you bring your bird in for a wing and nail trim.

A sick bird may be lethargic and therefore easy to handle in a towel, even if she isn't fully towel trained. A towel also has the advantage of keeping her warm, which is important with many illnesses.

plicated guillotine-type cutters are generally too large for a budgie.) Cut only the very tips of the nails, which consist of dead tissue similar to your fingernails; don't trim too far back, or you will cut into the quick. Keep styptic powder on hand to control those little accidents that can happen when a budgie flinches.

Diseases and Disorders

There are several very dangerous and deadly parrot diseases, but the likelihood of your captive-bred bird catching them is pretty rare, especially if you take certain precautions. Some diseases can be picked up in a pet store or by visiting another bird, can be passed on through the droppings of a pigeon or sparrow flying over an outdoor cage, or can even be caught through close contact between birds at a pet bird show. Regular visits to your veterinarian will help detect such diseases before they progress

This poor bird has a badly deformed beak and should not be purchased. The deformation may be the result of an injury or bad breeding, but the bird will not be able to eat properly and will not thrive without constant care.

too far. However, you still may find it helpful to know the symptoms for some common diseases.

Avian Polyomavirus

Once known as budgerigar fledgling disease, avian polyomavirus is a highly infectious disease that can be transferred among all species of parrots through sneezing, contaminated feces, feather dust, and food fed to young by infected adults. Typically, it kills nestling and weaning budgies, but it can also be carried in adults without symptoms. Infected birds stop feeding, bleed under the skin, regurgitate food, develop tremors, and die. To detect the disease, a veterinarian may take a cloacal swab; but if the virus is not actively shedding at the time the swab is taken, the results will be inconclusive. An alternative is a blood test: if the virus is detected, the bird definitely has the disease; but the bird may have the disease even if the virus does not appear to be present in the blood. Known carriers, of course, cannot be allowed to associate with any other parrots. There is no cure.

French Molt

French molt is a strange disease that sometimes attacks clutches of young budgies at the age when they should be leaving the nest. For some reason—opinions vary as to whether the condition is due to a virus, genetics, a parasite, or perhaps a nutritional deficiency—the primary feathers don't develop fully, growing in either short or twisted. The condition usually doesn't improve with later molts. Because the fledglings can't fly, they run instead. Although unsightly, budgies with French molt don't live shorter lives than normal budgies do; they just can't fly and use their wings correctly. You are unlikely to ever see a budgie with

French molt for sale at a pet store, but it could occur spontaneously if you breed your budgies. Never breed a budgie with French molt, because the disease may be passed on to the young.

Giardiasis

Giardiasis is a disease caused by the protozoan genus *Giardia*, which contains several species of intestinal parasites that are

Feather Picking

PARROTS ARE INTELLIGENT BIRDS WHO GET BORED easily, and they sometimes resort to plucking out their feathers out of boredom, much as you might bite your fingernails. Soon this activity becomes a compulsive habit, more and more time is spent picking, and the bird ends up with bare patches. Aside from making the bird unsightly, picking often causes serious sores and bleeding. If a budgie is picking at her feathers and skin, she may be suffering from an infection, a disease, or a nutritional deficiency. If someone in your household smokes, your budgie may be responding to the chemicals transferred from the smoker's fingers to her feathers and skin. Your veterinarian can determine any underlying medical problems.

Although feather picking isn't as common in budgies as it is in larger parrots, you should take steps to keep the habit from developing. First, check with your veterinarian to rule out disease. Then make sure her cage is large enough. Interact with your budgie several times a day, and give her lots of toys to keep her busy. Spending time on playgyms near their human companions often helps keep budgies too busy to even think of picking.

Giving a feather-picking budgie a companion to keep her occupied might seem like a good idea, but if the cause of the picking is a disease, the other budgie will also become infected. And if the other bird copies the behavior, the two budgies may pick each other!

common contaminants of food and water everywhere. In humans and most domestic mammals, minor *Giardia* infections cause diarrhea and nausea that soon pass with no serious problems, although children occasionally die from serious infections. One species, *Giardia psittaci*, can cause a fatal disease in young budgies and other parrots. The protozoan is spread through contaminated feces and water that come into contact with infected parrots, including parent birds. An infected young budgie cannot properly digest her food; even though she feeds heavily, she loses weight, plucks herself, screams, and is obviously uncomfortable. Eventually she dies. If detected early with blood work and other tests, giardiasis can be treated by a knowledgeable veterinarian. Giardia infections are common in budgies, so talk to your veterinarian about testing and routine treatment. Breeding birds should always be tested before being allowed to raise young; you don't want the parasite to spread to the chicks, and you don't want an already sick bird to be further stressed by breeding.

Newcastle Disease

Known also as avian pneumoencephalitis, Newcastle is a deadly and contagious disease. Caused by a virus, paramyxovirus-1, its first symptoms are sneezing and coughing; next are difficulties holding the wings and tail correctly, inability to walk, and strange head postures. Diarrhea and complete paralysis may follow, leading to death. Newcastle disease can rapidly spread through flocks of chickens and other poultry, causing millions of dollars in losses of adult birds, chicks, and developing eggs in just a week. Unfortunately, parrots are excellent carriers of Newcastle.

Because Newcastle can be an economically devastating disease, most states regularly check chicken flocks. State govern-

The wound on this budgie's wing is actually the spot where an incision was made to remove a tumor—another health problem your veterinarian would find during a regular examination.

ments also require that birds (including parrots) entering the state be quarantined if they don't carry health certificates declaring they aren't carriers. Parrots of many types have been carriers of the disease in the past, and in some parts of the country, veterinarians are under governmental orders to keep an eye out for Newcastle. Although this disease is preventable through vaccinations, the low cost of a budgie and the low chance that a pet store bird will carry Newcastle disease means that very few are vaccinated.

Pacheco's Disease

There are only a few obvious external symptoms of Pacheco's disease—such as diarrhea, ruffled feathers, and lethargy—and sometimes there are no symptoms at all. This virus is spread from parrot to parrot by common contact through sneezing, nasal discharge, and feces. It is often fatal, and birds who do survive become carriers who may continue to shed the virus. A vaccine exists, but some birds have shown negative reactions to it, so your veterinarian may advise against inoculation.

Avian Chlamydiosis (Psittacosis)

Psittacosis was once called parrot fever but is now more properly called avian chlamydiosis (because it attacks many bird species, not just parrots). This contagious disease is caused by the bacterium *Chlamydophila psittaci*, and it is one of the few bird diseases that can be transferred to humans. In humans, the disease is typically known as psittacosis. From 1988 to 2003, 935 human cases were reported to the U.S. Centers for Disease Control and Prevention. Once a dangerous human disease, psittacosis is now easily treated with antibiotics.

Humans usually pick up the bacteria by breathing infected dust from pigeon feces in old buildings and near park statues, not from parrots. In humans, psittacosis symptoms usually include a fever and chills that could progress to pneumonia and death if left untreated. Commonly, the heart muscles and liver become inflamed, leading to long-term health problems.

Your budgie could catch this disease if she is regularly kept outdoors in a cage where droppings from infected pigeons and house sparrows could contaminate her food and water. Your budgie can also contract psittacosis by being exposed to another pet bird with the disease. Psittacosis has few consistent signs in parrots other than bright lime-green droppings. It is detected most reliably by chemical and DNA tests of blood samples, and it is treated with a course of antibiotics. Unfortunately, an infected parrot does not gain immunity and can come down with the disease again.

Together, you and your avian veterinarian will help keep your budgie healthy and happy.

8

The Basics of Breeding Budgies

Before you decide to breed your budgies, think carefully about the commitment involved, and make sure you have homes for the all the offspring the breeding will produce.

BEFORE YOU DECIDE TO PUT YOUR PAIR OF BUDGIES together, carefully consider why you want to breed them. If you want to make money, you will surely be disappointed. The large pet store chains and even many local pet stores buy their birds from a well-organized network of breeders, wholesalers, and distributors who all closely control their overhead. They can sell a bird to a pet store for less than you spend to feed the parents during the nesting and weaning periods. You can't compete unless you have a stunning color variety, and even the most beautiful varieties sell for only a small premium over normal colors.

You must also consider the business aspects of selling your budgies. Businesses involving animals are subject to all types of legal requirements, from city and state business permits to inspection by state agricultural officials and health authorities. You will have to pay taxes and may have to pay some business-ownership fees. In some areas, you may not be allowed to breed birds for sale at all, so you will need to check zoning ordinances before you begin.

You may decide that you just want to breed a pair or two as a hobby, but have you thought about what you will do with perhaps eight to twelve young budgies after two breedings? Do you have the space to set up three or four very large cages to keep them as pets? Do you have enough friends and relatives interested in birds to adopt them? It's important that you don't bring new budgies into the world unless you are sure you can successfully place them in loving homes.

Sex Differentiation

If you have decided to breed a pair of budgies, the first step is to be sure you know the ages and sexes of the birds you plan to breed. Female budgies mature when only sixteen weeks out of the nest, and males mature at eighteen weeks (about five to six

It's easy to tell a mature pair of normal green budgies. Both have solid yellow heads, but the female (on the right) has a pale cere, whereas the larger male (on the left) has a tell-tale blue cere.

months old); they could breed at this point. You may have better success, however, if you give the young birds a chance to develop some muscle, store some fat, and strengthen their bones before breeding them. The first breeding should begin when the pair is roughly ten to twelve months old, no younger.

Visually determining the sex of a budgie is not as big a mystery as it is in so many other parrots. By the time they are five months old and have molted into their adult plumage, male budgies are easily recognized by their blue ceres. The blue can be pale or dark, depending to some extent on the individual and his hormonal levels, but it is always blue. Adult females have duller ceres that vary from tan (similar to that of an immature budgie) to bright pinkish. In older birds of both sexes, the ceres usually become wrinkled and rough in appearance, whereas they are smooth and shiny in younger adults.

Because budgies mature at such a young age and have such obvious differences in coloration, few people will pay for DNA sexing of immature budgies; instead, they wait until the birds molt into maturity. However, note that some color varieties don't display age differences in head coloration and may display only minor differences in cere color in adults. If you must be sure about the sex, ask your veterinarian to take a blood or feather sample, which can then be sent to a lab for DNA testing.

Selecting Parents

Responsible breeders won't breed related budgies, so purchase your birds from two breeders or pet stores that obtain their birds from different sources. Breeding closely related parents can concentrate defects (poor feathering, deformities, and poor personalities) in a line and reduce the fertility of the parents.

The adults should be healthy and should be free of parasite infestations, which means a visit to the veterinarian for checkups and fecal samples. The female especially should be eating well and taking a calcium supplement to ensure that she has sufficient fat and calcium reserves for laying. Select two birds who have good personalities. If either bird is trained to talk, expect that ability to be lost during and after breeding (especially for the female), and the bird may have to be retrained. The birds should be compatible, although they may have to be housed in adjacent cages for a week or two to get used to each other before putting them together. Almost as soon as they are placed in the same cage, the male will start courting the female, and eggs could follow in a few days.

Courtship and Mating

When introduced to each other, the female initially often ignores the male, who tries to court her. He sits next to her on the perch and whistles. He grooms her repeatedly and accepts

Nest Box

BUY THE LARGEST CAGE YOU CAN AFFORD FOR A *breeding budgie pair, preferably more than twenty-four inches in length. On one side of this cage, add a nest box purchased from a pet store—there is no reason to make your own, as commercial nest boxes, regardless of material, are inexpensive and reliable. Because the box will probably be thrown away after one breeding (they become extremely dirty, as you might expect), don't worry about investing in a durable box. Nest boxes for budgies generally are about ten inches long and six to eight inches high and have a perch under the opening.*

This is the beginning stage of the mating process. After mounting, the male typically wraps his wing around the female during copulation.

grooming in return. As things become serious, he offers the hen presents of bits of regurgitated food and tries to feed her. Most budgie couples hit it off fairly well at the onset, and there seldom is any fighting, so the pair often begins to mate in a matter of just one or two days.

Most pairs mate repeatedly. Young budgies often are rather clumsy when mating, and males may actually lose their footing and fall off the perch. Fortunately, it takes the two only a few attempts to learn the best ways to hold their bodies.

A mated pair of budgies will remain faithful for life if allowed to stay together. If the two birds are separated after several clutches to allow the hen to regain her strength, the two will recognize each other as soon as they again share a cage. The bond is easily broken, however, and breeders have few problems removing one bird of a pair and replacing the bird with a new male or female.

Egg Binding

Egg binding can be a serious and even deadly problem for the hen. Egg laying is very stressful to females, and it is quite common for the hen to produce defective eggs that don't have shells or have thin shells that are crushed while waiting in the oviduct to be laid. In such cases, the broken or poorly formed egg remains in the bird, who becomes obviously distressed, huddling in a corner with ruffled feathers and often not drinking. Breeders sometimes try to solve this egg-binding problem by adding a few drops of mineral oil into the vent, but this seldom works. Take an egg-bound female to the veterinarian immediately, or you may lose her. The veterinarian probably will give her an injection of calcium compounds and hormones to help the egg pass. And if

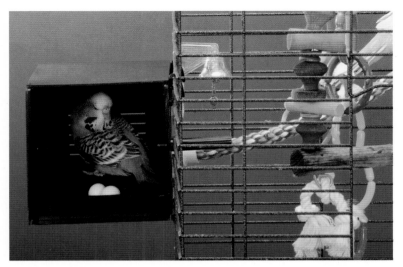

The female will lay her eggs in the nest box attached to the side of the cage. There she will stay for a few weeks while she incubates the clutch, and the male will feed her through an opening in the cage.

the egg breaks inside her, the veterinarian may have to perform minor surgery to remove bits of egg before they infect the oviduct.

Nesting

A hen may lay her first egg within a day or two of mating, followed by other eggs a day or two apart. Typical clutches are three to five white eggs. She usually starts to incubate the first egg before she lays the second, so there may be more than a week's difference in the hatching times of the young in a nest. The first egg hatches after eighteen days of incubation, whereas the fifth egg may hatch ten days later, assuming the eggs are laid at two-day intervals. This means that the first young to hatch are well developed before the last eggs even hatch. Fortunately, nature takes care of this problem by changing the feeding behavior of the older young; they need less food at night as they get older,

This young budgie is exercising his wing muscles, preparing to learn to fly and become fully weaned.

and so more food goes to the younger birds. Typically, budgies will raise all the hatchlings in a nest if given sufficient food.

As is typical of parrots, only the hen incubates the eggs (cockatiels are the exception: both parents brood and feed the chicks). She spends most of the day and night in the box, where she is fed by the male perched outside the opening. When she leaves the nest a few times a day to defecate, she passes large, soft blobs of feces compared with the usual small droppings. She also rolls the eggs several times a day. Incubating hens do not appreciate being disturbed on the nest, so just leave her alone. As the eggs begin to hatch after eighteen days, you may seldom see the hen while she keeps the nest warm and feeds the young.

After sixteen to seventeen days of incubation, the embryo in the egg is fully developed and begins to move about in the egg, placing his beak into the air pocket at one end of the egg. His lungs begin to function as his yolk sac is emptied and dries out, and he learns to breathe air that enters the egg through the porous shell. He makes circular motions with his head to help a tiny, sharp projection on the beak (the egg tooth) score a hole through the shell; that hole eventually allows the chick to first stick out his head and then completely break free of the egg. The mother budgie may help a chick leave the egg by chipping at the scored spot and rotating the egg to help the chick position himself. Hens hear the faint calls of the chicks while they are still in the eggs, so they know when the young are about to hatch.

The Nestlings

Baby budgies would certainly never win a beauty contest. They are hatched completely naked, with closed eyes and disproportionately large, blunt beaks. When fed by the mother, their crops become gigantic inflated food reserves, almost equal to the rest of their bodies in size. The chicks grow quickly, however, and by the time they are eleven days old, they are covered with down, and the first large feathers of their wings and tails are in place. The mother feeds them every one to two hours, day and night, for

Here is a youngster who hasn't yet had his first molt. Note the black banding on the head, the pale cere, and the dark eyes.

the first eight days; after that, she feeds them only during the day.

By the time the nestlings are four to five weeks old, they have full coats of feathers, and their muscles are developed enough to allow them to walk around the nest and even fly a bit. At this time, they leave the nest box but remain near it, and they are still fed by the parents for another week. During this period, they are usually called fledglings (emphasizing that they are learning to fly) or weanlings (indicating that their parents are weaning them to whole, unregurgitated seeds and a pelleted diet).

Hand-Raising Budgies

Budgie parents are usually allowed to raise their own young. The incubation period is short enough and the parents are diligent enough that there are seldom any problems, and so breeders just let the birds do the work. However, it is possible to remove the eggs from a nest and raise them yourself, although this is a complicated and time-consuming process.

Artificial Incubation

You will need an incubator that maintains a constant temperature of approximately one hundred degrees Fahrenheit for the

Budgies Mature Quickly

BABY BUDGIES HAVE THEIR FIRST FULL MOLT WHEN THEY are about four months out of the nest (five to six months from hatching). This is when they assume the adult coloration and have the ability to breed. This is extremely rapid development for a parrot—an adaptation to raise as many broods as possible in an environment where food and water are unpredictable.

If you plan to hand-raise the young from the beginning, you will need an incubator to maintain the eggs at a constant (very warm) temperature.

entire eighteen days of incubation. It should also be able to maintain a relative humidity of about 25 percent, rising to 50 percent just before the eggs start to hatch. Unless you can afford one of the most expensive types of incubators, you will have to turn the eggs at least six and as much as twelve times a day (ask an experienced breeder for advice) to prevent the developing embryo from sticking to the shell and becoming deformed or dying.

As a rule, breeders date the top of each egg with a soft wax pencil to indicate when it was placed in the incubator. This not only tells you how long the egg has been incubating but also gives you a reference point for turning it regularly. If necessary, you can remove eggs from the nest as they are laid and keep them in a moderately warm (sixty degrees Fahrenheit) cupboard for a few days until you are ready to place several in an incubator at the same time. The eggs will not develop at the lower temperature, but they will remain alive. Then you will have a brooder

Candling

BEFORE WASTING YOUR EFFORTS INCUBATING INFERTILE *eggs, you can examine them with a simple device known as a candler. A candler is a pinpoint source of strong light that illuminates the inside of the egg from the back while you look at the front. In a fertile egg, blood vessels develop within three days after incubation starts, and they cover more and more of the inside of the shell over time. These blood vessels become visible when the light passes through the egg. Infertile eggs remain clear (nothing develops) and never display the growing tissue. Candling devices can be made at home, but the light can be too hot and could damage the embryo—even with just a few seconds of use each day. Commercial devices are relatively inexpensive, and the best commercial candlers have bright but cool lights.*

with several hatchlings of the same age, regardless of when the eggs were actually laid.

When the chicks emerge from their eggs, place them in a brooder that holds a temperature of about one hundred degrees Fahrenheit. Next, you have to feed the chicks, which is truly the most difficult part of hand-raising birds.

Hand-Feeding Basics

Because there are too many details regarding hand-feeding to cover in a book this size, consider the information that follows to be a starting point. You will want to learn more from an experienced budgie breeder, your veterinarian, and a few good books on the subject. You'll find that there are many different opinions out there, so look for a breeder or veterinarian mentor you can trust and can count on if problems arise.

This older chick is being hand-fed a soft diet through a syringe. Hand-feeding is a time-intensive endeavor, and you may be better off letting the parents do the hard part and taking over near the end to establish your bond with the chick.

Unlike baby cockatiels, who have to be fed only during the day, baby budgies need food every two hours all through the day *and* night at first. This won't leave you much time for sleep. Special hand-feeding foods for nestlings are available at pet stores that cater to birds and through Internet and mail-order suppliers. There are many homemade formulations that work (often based on boiled egg mashes with supplements), but they can be complicated. It is best to use commercial mixes.

Many hand-fed babies are killed by improper feeding. The food must be fed at a consistently warm temperature, or the baby will not prosper. Commercial hand-feeding formulas may recommend temperature ranges specific to their brand and to the budgie's age. (Check the packaging for detailed instructions.)

Once your pair has finished raising the young, separate the two parents and begin to interact with them individually again. They will quickly remember their previous training and will once again be bonded to you.

Food that is colder than recommended will not be digested and will be regurgitated. Warmer food will burn the delicate lining of the baby's crop, resulting in a painful death. This means that you *must* use an accurate thermometer to measure food temperature.

When the baby is about eight days old, you can start reducing (and then cutting out) the nightly feedings and start spacing the daytime feedings a bit more widely apart. By the time the baby budgie is eleven days old, he can maintain his own body temperature better, and you can gradually start reducing the heat in the brooder; it should be roughly ninety degrees Fahrenheit by the time the bird is fully feathered.

If you try to raise your own baby budgies, expect many sleepless nights and many losses as well; it is probably best to just let the parents do it. You can cheat a bit, however, by removing a baby from the nest when he is three to four weeks old and almost fully developed, feeding him just during the day on a mix of fine pulp and some adult food. (For a full program, consult your veterinarian or a breeder experienced in hand-feeding.)

After Breeding

YOUR PET BUDGIES SHOULD NOT BE ALLOWED TO BREED more than once or twice, or you risk losing part of their friendly pet personalities to more natural budgie mentalities. Place the birds into their own cages, and begin to play with them on a regular basis again. Offer the usual treats and perhaps either try to teach them to speak or reinforce old tricks they may have forgotten. If you leave the pair together, the hen will continue laying clutch after clutch and could eventually die from low calcium levels—and simple exhaustion.

Because you have become the sole provider of his food and his only handler, the baby will bond strongly with you as a parent, and he will make a wonderful pet.

9
Some Budgie Color Mutations

Budgie breeders have developed a number of color varieties (called mutations), ranging from yellow to green to blue to white—and mixes of colors, too!

THE STUDY OF THE GENETICS OF BIRDS IS COMPLEX, AS their colors often are formed in different ways than just through pigments in the feathers and skin. The casual budgie owner interested in breeding a few budgies probably has little interest in the details of avian genetics, so this section will touch on it only lightly. Here you will learn how colors are formed in budgies and a little about a few major color varieties.

A Little Genetics

An animal (or plant, for that matter) inherits its characteristics through genes carried on chromosomes. Chromosomes are strands of DNA that form pairs, when in the cells of the body, and are single strands in eggs and sperm. Each DNA strand carries varying combinations of four amino acids that can pair with another acid on the other strand. These combinations produce proteins or enzymes that control how structures in the embryo will develop and when certain chemical processes will

English Budgies

ENGLISH BUDGIES ARE VERY LARGE (OFTEN TEN INCHES long or longer), bulky, big-headed budgies. They are popular with some owners who show their birds on a regular basis, and they are occasionally seen in pet stores. They owe their relatively gigantic build mostly to selective breeding over the past century, rather than to mutations. Breeders selected the largest birds of each clutch and then bred them to other very large birds, over and over again through the decades. English budgies show mostly the same color mutations as American (or common) budgies do, and the two can be interbred with no genetic problems.

This is a group of English budgies, who are larger and bulkier than their American counterparts but who also range in color.

This white bird has black accents and a bit of blue—not an albino, but a pretty color nonetheless.

Genetic Terms

GENETICS IS A COMPLEX SCIENCE, AND IT HAS DEVELOPED a complicated vocabulary to allow its practitioners to express themselves clearly. Although you will end up using few of these basic terms, you certainly will run across them if you delve deeper into budgie genetics.

- *Genotype: an individual's actual genetic makeup, as opposed to what is visible externally*
- *Phenotype: an animal's external appearance, as opposed to its genotype. Lutinos, for instance, are yellow birds, but several different genotypic combinations can produce birds who are externally identical.*
- *Dominant: a "strong" gene that overruns its weaker corresponding gene, the gene for green is dominant over the gene for blue.*
- *Recessive: the "weaker" gene of a pair controlling the same feature. Blue is the recessive of green.*
- *Allele: one of the two different versions of a gene at the same position on the chromosome strands. Usually one allele is dominant, the other recessive.*
- *Sex-linked: a trait carried on the chromosome with the genes that control sex. Male budgies have two large chromosomes (referred to as Z in birds and X in mammals), whereas female birds have one large Z (X) and a smaller W (Y) chromosome. The genes for some colors are found only the Z chromosome, so if a gene for a particular color occurs on the Z chromosome of a female, she will display that color. Albino and cinnamon are common sex-linked color mutations.*
- *Homozygous: a situation in which both genes controlling a character are the same, either both are dominant or both are recessive*
- *Heterozygous: a situation in which the genes controlling a character are different: one gene is dominant, and the other gene is recessive*

turn on and off. The differences among species are due largely to the sequences of these amino acids.

Mutations are inherited changes in the DNA, usually the result initially of high-energy rays of some type (such as cosmic rays or radioactivity) or of a strong chemical that changes the amino acid sequence, often by destroying one of the base pairs. If the cell survives the catastrophe, the offspring will carry the same defect. If the defect is not serious, the embryos will live and carry the mutation; when the animals mature, their offspring will have the ability to inherit the mutation as well.

Most mutations are neutral, having little or no effect on how the animal thrives. Many are harmful, preventing the embryo from developing and producing sex cells or preventing the sex cells from joining successfully in fertilization. Some mutations are deadly, killing the embryo in the egg or shortly after hatching. Only a few mutations are good in the sense of helping animals better adapt to their environments and giving them an advantage over other members of their population. For a budgie breeder, however, a mutation is almost exclusively one that changes the nature of the cells that produce the colors of a wild budgie. (In a few cases, it also changes other feather features, such as the development of small crests in some birds.)

Budgie Colors

What follows is a general explanation of how budgies get their different colors. There are exceptions, of course, and it is not possible to cover all the possibilities, so consider the following a primer in budgie coloration.

Although budgies are usually green, blue, or yellow, with black and white accents, there are really only two pigments in the

Budgies won't show all the color possibilities you can see in other birds because their skin and feathers have only two pigments: melanin (dark brown or black) and carotene (yellow, ranging to orange and red).

feathers and skin of budgies: melanin, a pigment that causes dark colors such as black and brown; and a carotene layer that produces yellow (varying to red and orange). Variations in color are caused by the way light travels through the carotene layer and is reflected or transmitted by the melanin layer. Carotene is located in the thin, transparent layer at the top of the color cells in the birds' feathers, whereas melanin granules are present toward the center of the cells.

The green and yellow colors we see in a normal green budgie are the result of the presence of pigments and the way the light absorbs and reflects the colors.

Normal Green

In a normal (wild type) green budgie, large amounts of melanin granules are present in the color cells, and the upper layer is translucent yellow from carotene pigments. After sunlight passes through the surface of the cell, the red part of the spectrum is absorbed by the melanin, but the blue wavelengths are reflected back through the surface. In the process, they must go through the yellow pigment layer. Our eyes see blue light filtered through yellow as green. A green budgie, remember, has a lot of melanin plus yellow in the surface layer. But because not all the cells of the body have a similar amount of melanin, we see yellow to yellow-green areas on the normal green budgie.

Blue

In blue budgies, there is a lot of melanin in the cells, but there is no yellow in the surface layer. Thus, when the blue light is reflected back from the melanin, it does not go through a yellow filter, and our eyes see blue. Remember: when melanin is present, yellow is absent.

Yellow

In yellow budgies, there is almost no melanin in the color cell, but the upper layer is yellow. Blue light passes through the cell and is not reflected, so all we see is the yellow of the surface layer. Remember: when melanin is absent, yellow is present.

White

As you might expect, white is the absence of both melanin and carotene pigments, with the upper layer of the color cells filled with reflective white granules. Most light waves pass through the

This pretty yellow budgie has no dark pigment and so has no dark coloration anywhere on the body. Pure yellow is very difficult to produce.

cell, but we see the white of the outer layer. Remember: white lacks both melanin and carotene.

Genetically Speaking

The presence or absence of the pigments is indicated by a short-hand code when geneticists and budgie breeders write about their birds. As a rule (some systems differ), genes that produce

Random matings will produce unique color patterns that defy classification and can't be accurately predicted. But that is part of the fun and excitement of breeding different color varieties.

Basic Mutations

melanin are indicated by O, those that produce yellow carotene by F. A green bird has both O and F genes, a blue only the O, a yellow only the F, and a white neither O nor F. The gene for melanin is carried on the Z (X) chromosome, so a male budgie may have one or two chromosomes with Z (X), a female only one. If the O gene is present in a female, it will be displayed.

As you might expect, these genes exist as dominant and recessive alleles, indicated by upper- and lowercase letters: F is dominant, f is recessive. A green bird might thus be indicated as FO, a blue one as fO, a yellow as Fo, and a white as fo. In reality, the details of inheritance of these simple factors are much more complicated; there are genes that control the intensity of the colors, for instance. Genes also occur in pairs, and one may be dominant and the other recessive.

Because of the complexity of the colors of budgies, it is difficult to generalize about what will happen when you mate two birds of similar or different colors, as the external appearance may not reflect the internal genetics. If homozygous birds are mated, their offspring will be the same color as the parents; if the

Here is an example of an albino budgie—a pure white bird with red eyes.

parents are heterozygous, a variety of different color distributions is possible, according to strict mathematical formulas.

Major Color Varieties

Currently, there are between seventy and one hundred recognized budgie color variations. However, many of these variations are simply differences in shade (dark green, light green) within larger variations (green versus blue, for instance). Another large number of recognized variations are rare and difficult to breed for, being found only at large budgie shows or exhibits. Still another significant number of variations are virtually impossible to distinguish without knowing something about the history of the budgies' parents and their genetics. Only the commonly seen colors are discussed in the following list.

- Albinos are all white, with no black (melanin) present in the feathers or skin. They have red eyes. This is a sex-linked mutation that is said to belong to the blue color series (yellow absent). Compare albinos with lutinos (of the green series).

- Blues have blue bodies and black and white striping in the wings. The face mask is white. Body color varies greatly, and three major shades of body color (sky blue, which is bright, clean blue; cobalt, which is deep cobalt blue; and mauve, which is a sometimes patchy purplish blue gray) are recognized.

- Cinnamons have pale, bright cinnamon brown in place of the black markings on the body and wings, and the brighter body colors are somewhat washed out. This mutation can be bred into any body color, such as cinnamon cobalt blue, cinnamon dark green, and so on. This is a sex-linked mutation said to be of the green color series (yellow is present).

- **Fallows** look a lot like cinnamons, but their shade of brown is darker, often with a bronzy tint. This mutation belongs to the blue series. To tell a fallow from a cinnamon (both can occur in all body colors and result in washed-out blues and greens), look at the eyes. A fallow always has dark red eyes, whereas a cinnamon chick has red eyes for only about a week after hatching; then the iris turns dark.

- **Greens** are perhaps the most commonly sold colors and represent small variations of the colors of wild budgies. The face mask is bright yellow (white in blues) and the body feathering is a shade of green. Three shades are recognized by most breeders: light green, dark green, and olive green.

- **Lutinos** are basically albinos belonging to the green color series. They are entirely yellow and have bright red eyes and red skin on their ceres and legs. Unlike albinos (who are white), lutinos don't all belong to the same mutation; there are sex-linked and non-sex-linked lutino mutations that appear identical externally. Together, lutinos and albinos are sometimes called inos.

- **Opaline** budgies have a V-shaped color design on their backs between their wings, and they don't have the fine, dark, curved feather edges seen in most other types of budgies. Opaline can occur as both blue and green variations and is sex-linked.

- **Violet** is an interesting mutation in which a gene intensifies the blue coloration to a deep violet shade. This dominant mutation is rarely seen.

- **Yellow** is another seldom-seen mutation because it is difficult to breed in a clean-looking form. Yellows look much like lutinos but differ in their genetics, and they often show patches of green feathering against the yellow.

This chapter only begins to scratch the surface of the color mutations of budgies, but it should be clear that these are exceedingly variable birds. More color variations are "discovered" all the time, and the number of technically different colors may be almost unlimited.

No matter what color your budgie is, with love and attention, she will be a treasured pet and companion for years to come.

Appendix

Budgie Societies

Budgie breeders and owners like to associate with others with similar interests, so there are many local budgie societies in the United States as well as in Canada, England, Europe, Japan, and Australia. In the United States, many local clubs are affiliated with an umbrella organization known as the American Budgerigar Society (http://www.abs1.org). Here, you will find listings for budgie clubs in many states and larger cities, almost certainly including one near you. Many clubs hold shows once or more each year and publish regular newsletters and even colorful magazines. One group, the Greater Western Budgerigar Society (http://www.gwbs.org), is noted for promoting the English budgie.

You also might want to check out the site of the American Federation of Aviculture at http://www.afabirds.org and the Parrot Pages at http://www.parrotpages.com for information on other clubs devoted to caged birds and many aspects of their care and breeding. *BIRDS USA* magazine (http://www.birdsusa.com) publishes an extensive list of bird clubs, including those dedicated solely to budgies.

FOSTER PARROTS, LTD.
http://www.fosterparrots.com
www.fosterparrots.com

THE GABRIEL FOUNDATION
http://www.thegabrielfoundation.org

NATIONAL PARROT RESCUE AND PRESERVATION FOUNDATION

http://www.parrotfestival.org

PARROT RESCUE INC.

http://www.parrotrescue.org

Glossary

albino: color mutation producing all white birds, with no black (melanin) present in the feathers or skin

blood feathers: new feathers just starting to emerge from their protective sheaths; these feathers have an active blood supply

bumblefoot: a swelling of the ball of the foot that may abscess

cere: the area of soft skin above the base of the beak that includes a budgie's nostrils

cloaca: the common opening in a bird through which the feces, urine, sperm, and eggs all pass; also called the vent

Convention on International Trade in Endangered Species (CITES): an intergovernmental agreement that regulates the importation and exportation of wild animals and plants

dimorphic: a physical characteristic that differentiates the sexes

egg tooth: a tiny, sharp projection on the beak that allows the chick to score a hole through the shell and eventually break free of the egg

fledge: to leave the nest and begin learning to fly

hypervitaminosis: a vitamin overdose

lutino: color mutation producing entirely yellow birds with bright red eyes and red skin on the ceres and legs

molt: the process of gradually shedding and replacing the feathers

monomorphic: lacking any physical characteristics that differentiate the sexes

mutations: changes in chromosomes that result in permanent changes that are inherited by offspring, such as color variations

opaline: color mutation producing birds with a V-shaped color design on their backs (between their wings) and lacking fine, dark, curved feather edges

preen: to groom the feathers with the beak

Psittacidae: the parrot family

psittacosis: an avian disease, more properly called avian chlamydiosis, that can be transferred to humans

uropygial gland (preen gland): the gland at the base of the tail that provides the oil birds use to groom their feathers

vent: the cloaca

wean: the period of growth in which the chick switches to an adult diet zygodactylous: a foot pattern that forms an X, with two toes in front and two in back

Index

A

accessories, cage, 55–67
allergies to budgies, 25
American Board of Veterinary
    Practitioners (ABVP), 101
avian chlamydiosis (psittacosis), 122
avian polyomavirus, 118
avian veterinarians, 101–103. *See also*
    veterinary visits
avoiding/detecting, 118

B

bathing cups, 60
beaks
    deformed, 117
    description of, 12
    inspecting, 40, 41
    trimming, 115
    use of, 73
behavior changes, 109–110
belly-up position, 92, 93
BIRDS USA, 101
Bird Talk, 101
biting, 89, 91
bleeding, 110–111, 113, 115–116
blood samples/tests, 104, 108
bonding/trust, 35, 83–85, 139
breeders, 39
breeding
    age, 127
    candling eggs, 137
    considerations before, 125–126
    courtship/mating, 128–130
    egg binding, 130–131
    egg laying, 18, 38, 131–133
    fledglings, 135
    hand-raising, 135–141
    incubation, 133, 135–137
    nesting, 131–133
    nestlings, 133–135
    parent selection, 127–128
    sex differentiation, 126–127
    weaning, 38, 44–45
    in the wild, 16–18
brooders, 137, 140
budgie societies, 159–160
business issues, 125–126
buying/selecting your budgie
    color selection, 33–35
    considerations before, 23–31
    health evaluations, 40–43
    males versus females, 35–36, 93
    number, 36–38
    personality, 9, 43–45
    weaning age, 38, 44–45
where to buy, 38–39

C

cages
    bathing cups, 60
    cleaning, 60–62
    costs, 26
    covers, 63
    flock size, 36–38
    food cups, 55–56
    introduction to, 47
    lighting, 62–63
    nest boxes, 128
    perches, 58–59
    placement, 52–55
    shape/construction, 48–52
    size, 48
    temperature, 17
    toys, 64–67
    water cups, 56–58
calcium, 128, 140
candling, 137
cere, 12, 27, 41
characteristics of budgies, 11–18, 27
choosing budgies. *See* buying/selecting
    your budgie
color varieties
    albino, 155
    blue, 150, 155
    choosing, 33–35
    cinnamon, 155–156
    fallow, 156
    genetics of, 143–147, 152–155
    lutino, 156
    mutations, 14, 21
    normal green, 150
    opaline, 156
    violet, 156
    white, 150, 152
    wild budgies, 13–15
    yellow, 150, 156–157
contagious diseases, 102
Cook, Captain James, 18–19
costs, 26, 108, 110

D

dangers
    bleeding, 27, 113
    cages, 50
    chemicals/cleaners, 58–59, 61
    children, 28–29
    cold/hot food, 140
    drafts, 54
    flight, 67, 112
    grit, 79
    household/kitchen, 54
    other pets, 29–31
    over-breeding, 140
    smoke, 27–28

spreading infection, 40
sudden movement, 27
toys/playgyms, 65–67
during training, 87
trimming nails/beaks/feathers, 110,
  111, 113, 115–116
unsafe foods, 78–79
vitamins, 76
diarrhea, 40, 42, 71, 105, 120, 121
diet/feeding
  breeding females, 128
  calcium/cuttlebones, 80
  fat, 69
  fruit/vegetables, 71–72
  grit, 78–80
  hand-feeding, 44–45, 83, 137–141
  human foods, 78
  laying females/sick birds, 75
  nutritional deficiencies, 99
  pellets, 69, 70–71
  routines, 80–81
  seeds, 69, 72–76
  supplements, 76
  water, 81
  weaning, 38
diseases/disorders. See also veterinary
    visits
  avian chlamydiosis (psittacosis), 122
  avian polyomavirus, 118
  avoiding/detecting, 116, 118
  beak problems, 115, 117
  bleeding, 110–111, 113
  contagious diseases, 102
  diarrhea, 40, 42, 71, 105, 120, 121
  egg binding, 36, 130–131
  emergencies, 110–111
  examinations, 100–101
  feather picking, 119
  French molt, 118–119
  hypervitaminosis, 71
  Newcastle disease, 120–121
  nutritional deficiencies, 99
  obesity, 72
  Pacheco's disease, 121–122
  respiratory, 27
DNA, 143–147
droppings, 42

E
egg binding, 36, 130–131
eggs. See also breeding
  incubation, 131–133, 135–137
  infertile, 137
  laying, 18, 38, 130–131
emergencies, 36, 110–111. See also
    diseases/disorders; veterinary visits
English budgies, 12, 144
exercise, 57, 99
eyes, 14, 40, 41

F
face, 13–14
feathers
  blood feathers, 27, 111, 113
  feather picking, 119
  inspecting, 40
  wild budgies, 12, 13, 14
  wing feathers, 42, 67, 111–115
fecal samples, 105, 107
feeding. See diet/feeding
feet, 12–13, 42, 43
females versus males, 35–36, 93
financial considerations, 26
finger training, 85–89
fledglings, 135
flight, 67
flight feathers, 111–115
food cups, 55–56
French molt, 118–119

G
genetics, 143–147, 152–153
giardiasis, 119–120
glossary, 161–163
Gould, John, 19

H
habitat in the wild, 16
handling, 27, 45. See also training
hand-raising basics, 44–45, 83, 135–141
head, 13–14
health. See diseases/disorders; veterinary
    visits
health certificates, 102
heart rate, 103
history of imports, 18–21
humidity, incubation, 136
hypervitaminosis, 71

I
imported birds, 102
incubation, 131–133, 135–137
infertile eggs, 137

L
legal issues, 26–27, 102
legs, 42
life span, 45
lighting, 62–63

M
males versus females, 35–36, 93
mating, 128–130. See also breeding
metabolism, 103
minerals, 80
molting, 114–115, 118–119, 135
mutations, color, 14, 21. See also color
    varieties

N

nails, 43, 115–116
names, scientific/species, 10, 11, 19
nest boxes, 128
nesting, 131–133
nestlings, 133–135
Newcastle disease, 120–121
nutritional deficiencies, 99

O

obesity, 72, 99, 105
oil glands, 12

P

Pacheco's disease, 121–122
parasites, 119–120
parent-raised babies, 44
parrot family, 9–11
pelleted diets, 70–71
perches, 58–59, 89
perches/perch training, 91
personality, 9, 43–45
pets, household, 29–31
pet stores, 38–39
picking feathers, 119
playgyms/toys, 64–67
poultry diseases, 102
preen gland, 60
psittacosis (avian chlamydiosis), 122

Q

quarantines, 102, 121

R

range in the wild, 16
regurgitation, 130
rescue groups, 39
respiratory problems, 27, 40, 111. See also
    diseases/disorders

S

scientific names, 9–11, 19
seeds, 69, 72–76
selecting your budgie. See buying/select-
    ing your budgie
sex
    choosing, 35–36, 93
    identifying, 127
    sexual maturity, 135
shelters, 39
sippers, 57
size
    of budgies, 11–12, 105
    of cage, 48
    of flock, 36–38
    skin, 42
step up/down training, 87–89
substrates, cage, 52
supplements, 71, 76, 80, 128

T

talking, 35–36, 92–95
taming, 44
temperature
    brooders, 137, 140
    cage/room, 17
    food (hand-feeding formulas), 138,
        140
    incubation, 135
    normal body, 103
terminology
    genetics, 146
    glossary, 161–163
toes, 43
towel training, 90–92, 107, 116
toys, 64–67
training
    belly up, 92, 93
    bonding/trust, 83–85, 139
    finger, 85–89
    males versus females, 35–36
    perch training, 89, 91
    talking, 35–36, 92–95
    towel, 90–92, 107, 116
    tricks, 95–97
transportation/travel, 102, 111
trimming
    beaks, 115
    nails, 115–116
    wing feathers, 111–115
trust/bonding, 35, 83–85, 139

U

ultraviolet lights, 62

V

vacations, 26
veterinary visits. See also diseases/disor-
    ders
    beak trimming, 115
    checkups, 43, 91, 100–101, 103–110
    costs, 26, 108, 110
    emergencies, 110–111
    examinations, 43, 91, 93, 100–101,
        103–110
    fecal samples, 105, 107
    finding a veterinarian, 100–103
        health certificates, 102, 121
    nail trimming, 115–116
    transportation, 111
    yearly exams, 107–108
vitamins, 71, 76

W

water, 56–58, 81
weaning, 37, 38, 44–45
Web sites, budgie societies, 159–160
weight, 99, 105
wild budgies, 11–18
wings/wing feathers, 42, 67, 111–115